Mussels
At
Midnight

The Autobiography
of
Captain Stephen Anderson

Christian Focus Publications

© Stephen Anderson 1989

ISBN 0 906731 93 3

Published by

Christian Focus Publications Ltd

Tain   Houston
Ross-shire   Texas

Christian Focus Publications is a non-denominational
publishing house. The views expressed are these of the
authors.

Printed and bound in Great Britain

CONTENTS

MILESTONES

1927	Stephen Anderson born
1935-1944	School
1944-1957	Army

	Joined Regiment	1946
	ADC Germany	1949-1950
	ADC Middle East	1950-1952

1957-1969	Farming

	Converted	1963
	Call to be Evangelist	1968
	(Edinburgh Mission)	

1969-1987	Evangelist

	Move from Edinburgh to Aviemore	1974
	Scotroc	1980-1987
	Shetland Mission	1984
	Malawi	1985

Foreword By William Still

Having read through my friend Stephen Anderson's Autobiography several times, as well as knowing him well as to his present character, I feel I can sum up something of the nature and impact of his life on the Scottish religious scene, especially since the Second World War.

It will be more than a surprise to those who know Stephen only in the severe domesticity of a congregational mission or in intimate personal chat, to learn of his background. For, despite his modesty about his attainments from childhood, he became captain of his prestigious school, Glenalmond; received the Sword of Honour at Sandhurst on passing out as a young officer; was appointed A.D.C. to the General Commanding the Army of Occupation in Germany; served in Africa and became Adjutant to his regiment; and as son of a wealthy Scottish landowner had access to the elite of his day, associating constantly with the high in the land, including polo at Cowdray Park with Prince Philip and dancing with the Queen at a grand ball in Edinburgh.

Into this pleasure-loving life of sport and high society came a Christian girl, Joy, whom in the divine economy he was attracted to naturally, but found her firm faith in Christ something of an embarrassment. This created a tension in Stephen's life and produced a turmoil which, albeit ending happily in his conversion, the tension was perpetuated in the high-spirited fellow being catapulted into a new sort of society, one whose Christian faith cut across, although it did not ignore class distinctions. To find his feet and his vocation in this new way of life has involved him on a variety of phases.

He left the army and returned to farming on the family

estate; but becoming increasingly involved in evangelistic work was appointed lay evangelist to the Church of Scotland, eventually establishing Ski Centres for Evangelism. During the years Stephen has been engaged in various sorts of mission work as an itinerant evangelist, organising local teams and generally seeking to stir up the Church towards responsibility for the evangelising of our supine Church and increasingly godless nation.

He has suffered for his pains in many directions and at the hands of many, being sometimes vastly misunderstood; but he has never been deflected from his vision, even at the time of his sorest affliction, at Aviemore. One of his daringest ploys was Scotroc, an evangelistic team using music and drama which did brave work in various places, including abroad, to the chagrin of some, the amusement of others, but to the blessing of not a few way-out souls.

His next and present assignment, to his great surprise, was to become associate minister with David Anderson at Gorgie, Edinburgh, lately come from a fruitful ministry in Bainsford, Falkirk.

Nonetheless, one wonders, how many phases this man of action and creativity will yet to through ere he sees the Gospel flourish in the land he loves and covets for Christ? For perhaps Stephen's most significant activity so far has been in connection with the forward-looking movement called Concern for Scotland, by which he seeks to cover the whole land with prayer for revival and for the renewal of godliness in Scotland.

What, then, has been Stephen Anderson's place in the religious life of Scotland during these last forty years? He has seen the Presbyterian Church which, during the first thirty years of this century was undoubtedly in the doldrums due to the vast spread of liberal influences, united in 1929. The cross-fertilisation which was ensued by this Union brought at least remnants of the Gospel to congregations which had never heard it; and the rise of Christian Unions of the Inter Varsity Fellowship in our Universities ultimately influenced a considerable number of Church of Scotland young people. Furthermore, with such 'charismatic' spirits as D.P. Thomson and Tom Allan on the go, the Gospel began to become respectable again in Church of Scotland circles.

But not to the extent that when Stephen Anderson came on the scene with a sense of reality which forbade him calling a spade anything but a spade, there arose a huge objection to his methods and views, not only among the Establishment (it took seven years for his name to appear as lay evangelist in the Year Book!), but among congregations who had never heard anything like this plain Gospel.

Yet through the years, this man of God has steered a course which although it may have looked somewhat zig-zag at times, yet has been quite single-minded as to his ultimate aim. He has therefore emerged more than anyone else in Scotland as a man combining a passion for evangelism with a burden for prayer which in its effect and influence may very well turn out to be the most significant thing to happen to the Church of Scotland this century. He has been the freshest breath of fresh air to blow through the Church of Scotland for a long time.

I have been fascinated and deeply challenged by my brother's life story.

I would not want to be out of step with him in his burden for our land. Maybe the Church will yet share this view, and be prepared to follow where he has led. Amen!

William Still.   19.9.89

Chapter 1

SPORT, SOCIETY AND SUCCESS...BUT

They tell me I was born with a silver spoon in my mouth: I always thought that must be extremely painful for both baby and mother. But I suppose in reality it means that my parents were considered to be very well off.

My father had been in the tea trade in India so that when I was born, the fourth of the family, we had an estate in Perthshire and a London house. My father was at that period spending more and more time in Scotland, which was to become the scene of my upbringing. According to him, because of his connection with India, I was due to be the Viceroy of that country, but in fact a war and various other obstacles, such as the fact that four hundred and fifty million Indians decided that they no longer wanted a Viceroy, made sure I did not fulfill that destiny.

I attended a preparatory school in England for the accepted statutory four years just before the war and I suppose thought as much or as little about life as any other boy of eight-to-twelve years. One abiding memory I have is that of intense disappointment - and indeed resentment - when I was left out of the football eleven; I considered that I was far better than a number of those who had been included. This passion for sport was something that characterized my life. When at home in Scotland, I revelled in shooting and other outdoor activities.

At the advent of war in 1939 I was sent, as a thirteen-year-old to Trinity College, Glenalmond, a public school offering a monastic existence in a very beautiful but isolated part of Perthshire. Again I have little memory of events which were to have a radical effect on my life, but I suppose one or two incidents were pointers to what lay ahead.

I remember, for instance, being bullied when I was in the middle school, probably because I was very insufferable, and thought that a certain amount of wealth gave me the right to order others about: this is never popular in a group of boys. The result was that I became very unhappy and had virtually no friends, apart from one young man who had also suffered the same sort of treatment but was rather tougher than I was, both in spirit and body. I remember being amazed when he dropped a note into my spartan little room, which was the form of accommodation provided for the pupils. On that note there were written some words from the Bible saying: 'Greater love hath no man than this, that a man lay down his life for his friends'. I am not quite sure what he meant by it, and it certainly had little effect on me at the time, but it is a memory that lingers with me to this very day.

Towards the end of my public school days things changed quite a lot and I very much enjoyed my time there. I remember that in the last year I was the only person doing modern languages in the sixth form. My total academic education during that period took place on a Tuesday evening when I had to report to my housemaster, who was a notable eccentric.

From ten o'clock at night until three, four or even

six o'clock the following morning we sat over innumerable cups of coffee and discussed some of the books that we had been given to read. When we talked about French books, we talked in French; when it was German literature, then we spoke in German; when the books were in Spanish, that was the language used.

It was an unusual education but it certainly helped me to have a broad outlook, and perhaps rather an adult approach to life. I was privileged to be the Captain of the school during my last year and one of the memories that comes back to mind is that I was not made the Captain of rugger during my last Winter season. That rankled very considerably. It was the same sort of attitude that had prevailed in the preparatory school a few years before. Looking back, I see just how powerful and damaging a spirit of resentment and envy can be.

One of the features of Glenalmond was that, it being a Church of England school, chapel was held twice daily. Frankly, memory of it was of medieval religion, and the only service that I can recollect was when a young man set off an alarm clock in the middle of one of the sermons. The thing that struck me particularly was that, when every head in that chapel turned towards the lad, he turned round and looked at the boy behind. It was that boy who landed in trouble. Such were the memories of religion at school. Habits, however, are formed, and because I had been encouraged to go to church by my mother and then again at school, this continued when I began my army career.

I am sure that Bernard Castle must have been one

of the coldest spots in Britain that January of 1944. As a trooper in the Royal Armoured Corps I was treated as rather less than human, and yet there was a certain sense of adventure which made those dreary days exciting and memorable.

I had volunteered for the army at seventeen-and-a-half years of age, mainly I must admit to avoid being called up, because I knew as a volunteer I would have the choice of which branch of the army I wanted to enter, and I had always been determined to be in the Cavalry or Armoured Corps. Before long I was asked to go on a short course at Oxford University in order to train as a potential officer. This, I reckoned would be a great experience, and I accepted.

I found on arrival that I was expected to do academic subjects in the morning - chemistry and physics, which I had never done at school. I went to one or two of the lectures and found them totally incomprehensible: after all, I had never done the basics. As a result I simply did not bother to go to the lectures in the morning but assiduously attended all the military subjects in the afternoon. I claim to be the only person who has ever scored zero in an Oxford examination but at the same time passed out top of the military subjects! Consequently I was encouraged to go to Sandhurst as a potential officer in the Royal Scots Greys. At that course I obtained the Sword of Honour and left to join my regiment towards the end of the war in Europe.

Sport was still very much the centre of my life. I played rugger, cricket and tennis, and I skied and boxed. I have clear memories of one incident which I now see as having deep spiritual significance. I was boxing against the middle-weight champion of the Marines and towards the end of the first round I caught him with a really effective right hook. He went down with this and was only saved by the bell. He knew and I knew, the referee knew and our seconds knew that in fact the fight was over although the man came out for the second and third rounds. During those rounds he tried every dirty trick in the book. I was fortunate in having had good training from my instructor and so was duly declared the winner. Looking back I see the strong resemblance between that fight and the fight against evil in the life of a Christian, where Satan has already been defeated by Jesus Christ on the Cross at Calvary and yet he comes out knowing that his time is short and fights with every dirty weapon in his possession.

When you are young, the army offers a tremendous career and great opportunities for living abroad and in a style which would be impossible in any other sphere. Certainly, at the end of the war I had opportunities to take part in sports and other activities in the army which I would never have had in civilian life.

The Army of Occupation, of which my regiment formed a part, was almost totally divorced from the German nation, with whom we mixed with only very occasionally. It was in many ways a false life. We ignored a great deal of what was going on around us and lived lives of luxury where material possessions were very easy to come by. Whisky was six and eight pence, or thirty-four new pence, a bottle and there were no shortages. We used to be able to afford to play polo, shoot and go ski-ing at extremely cheap rates, whereas many of the Germans were almost at starvation point.

The contact that we made was at Belsen, which was being used as a displaced persons' camp. My regiment was on guard when a raid for black market goods was carried out and I remember seeing a room, big enough to take six cars, absolutely full of tins of coffee, each tin being worth about fifty pounds in German currency. The contrast between my life of luxury and the sordid squalor of the black market, under the shadow of the gas chambers, struck home, but was quickly dismissed.

I remember, too, a friend turning up with a Rolls Royce which had been found under a haystack, and another finding a very special combined rifle and gun worth many hundreds of pounds, which had been hidden in a potato clamp. For the cost of one blanket and a packet of cigarettes, I bought myself a rough-haired German dachshund with a pedigree as long as my arm.

Before long I was appointed ADC (or Aide-de-Camp) to the British General who was High Commissioner at the time. This meant that he was virtually dictator of the British Zone in Germany, and being his ADC gave me considerable power. I was in charge of the social and domestic aspects of his life which included having charge of two castles as well as a private aeroplane, train and four cars.

On one occasion the High Commissioner was to meet with his Russian counterpart in Berlin. It gave me great pleasure to telephone the German railways and order the private train - which incidentally had belonged to Goebbels and included a bar, lounge and bathroom. I ordered the senior railway executive to have the train ready within half an hour and to phone me back within ten minutes with a schedule of its route to Berlin through the Russian zone. The resultant deferential 'Jawohl, Herr Hauptmann' did a great deal to boost my ego and confirm the high opinion I had of myself.

Another incident involving transport now causes me to laugh as well as blush. We had a Rolls Royce, with a V12 engine, capable of doing 125 mph on the German autobahns. The American equivalent was a fairly ancient Cadillac and their High Commissioner's ADC was constantly eyeing the Rolls with envy. On one occasion, however, he asked me to come across and see their new car. It was a brand new Cadillac, a magnificent looking vehicle with almost everything electrically operated. He showed me around, and I have to admit that I was green with envy as he pressed this button to open the windows and that button to operate the air conditioner, and so on. Eventually in a very superior tone he offered me a ride. Reluctantly, but with a forced smile on my face, I agreed. He pressed the starter and nothing happened. The battery had been exhausted with all the electronic devices!

I stepped out with a sense of intense superiority and delight at my colleague's discomfiture. It was many years before I was to read and grasp the implications of the Scripture which speaks of rejoicing with those that rejoice and weeping with those that weep. That US ADC must have felt rotten!

My boss was then appointed as the Commander-in-Chief Middle East Land Forces based in Egypt and he asked me to serve an extra term as an ADC in order to help him over the move from Germany. We now lived on the shores of the Great Bitter Lake in the central stretch of the Suez Canal area, and the whole of Egypt was open to us. His responsibilities stretched from Gibraltar to Aden and from Turkey to Cape Town. As his personal staff officer I had to know what was going on and make all the arrangements for his day-to-day living and any travelling that had to be done.

A number of incidents from those days stand out in mind. I remember well the night when an operation had been planned to take over the island of Abadan in the Persian Gulf, because the ruler was causing difficulties with our oil supplies. Just on midnight, prior to the launching of the attack at dawn, I received a telephone call direct from 10 Downing Street. I had to waken the General, who was told to cancel the attack at some six hours notice. Again the feeling of importance at being in such a position did much to confirm my high self-esteem.

Whilst in Egypt I was asked by the General, who was as keen a polo player as I was, to go to Jordan and buy two ponies for each of us. I was treated with great respect by the Jordanian Army, who had lined up a considerable number of ponies and suggested that I play one or two chukkas on each of the ponies they had selected. The ground was uncleared desert and the ponies were totally untrained and indeed unbroken.

8

The result was a truly hair-raising afternoon.

In the midst of it all, two of us collided and the other man fell off and broke his neck on the rocky desert. The sort of situation that arose under those circumstances can perhaps be imagined. And yet, despite the shock, I had no real awareness of the fact that I had killed a man, and returned to Egypt as if very little had happened: I was almost more concerned about getting the ponies transported across the Red Sea. In some ways, this attitude was perhaps attributable to the fact that death was by now all around us. The King of Egypt had abrogated the treaty with Britain and so we were living in a small enclave called the Canal Zone. We were surrounded by Egyptians who were entirely hostile and yet we were still involved in the whole community. We had to be armed at all times and were never sure whether the man serving the soup might not be ready to plunge a knife into our backs at the same time.

One morning when I was going to collect a new armoured vehicle for the Commander-in-Chief I was ambushed and blown up by a petrol bomb under the jeep. This got on to the BBC news, and my family were unsure whether I was dead, a hero, or just a bit shaken. It was on that occasion, as we lay in the ditch by the road, with bullets flying over our heads, that I heard the really pagan sergeant next to me letting out the most fervent prayer - 'Oh, God! Get me out of here!' I admit I was echoing that prayer, but like him certainly never gave any thanks to God when we were delivered.

Travelling throughout the Middle East was

thrilling, and to be involved in top-level discussions of a strategic nature with people as far apart as Syria and South Africa all helped to add to my tremendous sense of importance and excitement.

There were some very beautiful sights, too, which will stay with me forever. Over the Hindukush is a pass called the Ruwanduz which is one of the most magnificent and beautiful in that glorious part of the world. I saw the sun rise over Mount Kenya and literally thousands of hippos and crocodiles ducking beneath the waters of the Thomson Falls as our aircraft skimmed a hundred feet above them.

These experiences, however, registered merely as a sign of the 'Good Life' and I gave little thought to the Creator. Any idea of a personal relationship with a living God was far from my thoughts at the time. I was still going to church but my church-going had no effect upon my day-to-day living. Perhaps the story of our journey to South Africa illustrates this.

I was responsible for making all the arrangements. We were going by the private plane that was placed at the disposal of the Commander-in-Chief by the Royal Air Force, and the party consisted of the General, his batman (who would be needed to make sure that the frequent changes of uniform necessary would go without a hitch) and myself as aide. When we arrived in Nairobi, I found to my horror that the batman had no valid yellow fever inoculation certificate. I should have checked this but had failed to do so. He was told that he would not be allowed into South Africa. In consternation I went to the officials and asked what could be done; I certainly did not relish the prospect of telling my General that I had failed in my job. The official looked at me and said, 'Oh, we can give him an injection at the airport but it will be ten days before he will be allowed to travel'.

I arranged for him to get the inoculation and then carefully forged the certificate so that he could continue on that journey, knowing perfectly well that I was putting at risk a considerable number of Africans, yellow fever being fatal to the African population. Nevertheless, the next day I was in church singing lustily as usual. Religion and reality were far removed from each other in my thinking and my life.

These attitudes began to change, however, when I left the job of ADC and returned to my regiment, which was stationed in Barce in North Africa. It was at this point I met the girl who was later to become my wife, and discovered that for her Christianity was not just a religion but a way of life which affected everything about her. I found her extremely attractive and courted her over two thousand miles. Whenever I managed to get home on leave I was much in her company, although I have to admit that I was taking out another girl on alternate weekends. Eventually I had to choose between them and committed myself to Joy, who has been my wife for thirty-five years. As a Christian she knew that she should not marry me but persuaded herself that my churchgoing meant that I was really a Christian at heart. God was gracious enough to resolve the situation but we would both now firmly agree that it is wrong for a Christian to marry outside the living faith and that our case was the exception which only proves the rule.

We were married on a Tuesday, and left for Austria by car on the Wednesday with our eventual destination as Barce in Libya, via Tunis. We were due to spend two weeks ski-ing in Austria and arrived at our Hotel covered in confetti. Having driven all the way from Calais we lay exhausted and to our consternation broke the bed. I can still remember the embarrassment with which I approached the Hotel keeper to tell him that we, a honeymoon couple, had just broken the bed!

But worse was still to come because on the following morning, when I took my wife to the top of the nursery slopes and suggested she should ski down, I was met with a blank refusal. I had skied virtually all my life, including a three months course of winter warfare with the Norwegian Army on the Arctic Circle, and she had done only three weeks. To her the slope that faced her was ridiculously steep and she flatly refused to attempt it. Our first row took place on the top of the nursery slopes at St Anton and might have lasted a lot longer had it not been so cold. Eventually we arrived at Barce and she moved into a small flat in the Arab quarter, where she was left alone for many hours of the day whilst I was committed to the army work. Looking back on it, I cannot think how she survived; perhaps because it was two thousand miles to go home to mother!

I was heavily committed to my career at this stage and had been made the Adjutant of my regiment: the promotion involved a great deal of work. I do clearly remember learning one thing about leadership at this point. My Commanding Officer was a small man who never raised his voice and indeed seemed totally incapable of imposing his will upon anyone; yet I knew that he had won a DSO and an MC, and held a Gold Medal from the three-day event in Helsinki. That small, insignificant-looking man had such qualities of leadership that most of us would gladly have died for him.

I began to see that in reality there was more to power than strength or force, and related this to the fact of my wife's powerful Christianity. Despite all that, I was not prepared to consider any commitment to Christ for myself at this stage - I was far too keen on promotion in my chosen career and on enjoying life and sport.

One experience from those days means so much to me now. I was left behind as the Rear Officer of my regiment when we moved back to Crookham in England. My wife and son had to return with the regiment and I was living by myself in a small hut for two or three months, making sure that everything was tidied up before we finally handed over. I remember vividly that half of my mind was where my wife and young son were. That did not prevent me from working as hard as I possibly could in order to get things cleared up, but in reality half of me was not in Barce but in Crookham. Now, I see it as a tremendous illustration of the Christian's living his life on this Earth and yet half of him is with Christ in Heaven.

But for me Heaven was, at that time, more the thought of getting back to England and having at least one season of polo whilst I could still afford it. Cowdray Park was not far from Crookham and on arrival there I was able to keep two ponies and play at least once per week. I was asked to join a very good team, mainly because my handicap was helpful to them, and I found myself often playing against Prince Philip and other notables.

Life seemed to be completely full, and yet there was frustration: I found that the army life was beginning to pall and that I was resenting the authority and becoming increasingly discontented. The crucial point was reached when I was told that, although I had passed the exam for the staff college, I had been two days too young and therefore would have to take it again. Partly in a fit of temper, partly because we now had two children to support and partly because the tenant of the estate in Perthshire was giving up, I decided to leave the army and move to Straloch to farm what had been my father's estate there.

My last job as a soldier was to organise Her Majesty the Queen's visit to my regiment, and to plan a ball to be held in the Assembly Rooms, Edinburgh. Because I had organised the whole event, I was privileged to dance with Her Majesty at the ball, and found to my consternation that she wanted to go into the second ballroom, whereas I had been prepared to dance a Scottish Reform with her in the main room.

To my horror the band was playing a Charleston, a dance which I had never seen or attempted in my life, and here was I faced with the prospect of doing it with the Queen. Her Majesty danced with great skill, although I noticed that she found it quite difficult to keep the tiara on her head. My own feelings are perhaps best left to the imagination. Nevertheless, it was quite a climax to an army career, and I left, if not in a blaze of glory, at least with a feeling of achievement and a job well done.

The estate that I inherited from my father had been farmed by a tenant who had neither the resources nor perhaps the energy to make the most of it. I was therefore faced with the daunting prospect of running a farm that needed thirty miles of fencing, almost complete restocking, and a vast amount of work to be done on the buildings.

I have never worked so hard as during those first two years, and being by nature something of a workaholic it meant that family relationships deteriorated rapidly. This was aggravated, after two years, by the fact that the owner of the neighbouring estate of some seventeen thousand acres was looking for a manager and I was invited to take on this task. As a result I was farming in all over twenty-five thousand acres of hill land.

Outwardly everything seemed to be going extremely well. The farm was on the up and up, the neighbouring estate improved its performance, and I found myself elected to the branch and area committees of the National Farmers' Union. Money was not scarce, and as well as working long hours I was able to enjoy a number of days off for shooting and ski-ing holidays, both abroad and in neighbouring Glenshee. Most of my neighbours would undoubtedly have cast envious eyes towards me and thought that I had everything that was required for a contented life; but I knew that there was something missing. I could scarcely define it, and looked for it in working hard,

in playing hard and, I have to admit with great
reluctance, in looking around at members of the
opposite sex, one of whom responded in a way that
ensured that our family life was at a very low ebb.

It was at this stage that my wife invited some
students from the Bible Training Institute in Glasgow
to stay for a long weekend. I found something very
attractive in these young people who seemed to enjoy
themselves to the full without recourse to alcoholic
stimulant. By this time I was drinking a considerable
amount, and as I sat by the fire with a large tumbler of
whisky at my side it amazed me to see others able to
enjoy themselves in a way which, reluctantly, I rather
envied. At the same time there was something about
them that really annoyed me. They were so sure of
their Christian faith. They spoke of knowing God. I
felt inferior and my anger was aroused. I was aware
already of this type of experience because my wife's
faith challenged me - and no man likes to feel inferior
to his wife!

And so these young people brought to the surface
the two emotions which had been simmering in me
with regard to Christianity: there was a clear
attraction, but at the same time a strong feeling of
antagonism.

It was not many weeks later that my wife invited me
to accompany her to her mother's home to hear an
evangelist who was going to address a small meeting
in the drawing-room. Just imagine it: here was I not
getting on with my wife but invited to hear an
evangelist speak at my mother-in-law's! However,
rather than risk another row with my wife, I decided

to attend, thinking that I could switch off my mind and make plans for the following day's work of gathering the sheep. I remember being somewhat embarrassed in that drawing-room because I was the only one smoking, and as the evangelist, Leith Samuel, began to speak I did not know what to do with my cigarette. I started to let my mind wander on to sheep but to my amazement found that I had to listen.

This man spoke in a way that was different from any other 'professional' Christian that I had heard before. He spoke of sin in a way which made it quite clear to me that this was not only a personal, internal attitude common to us all but also that it was the root cause of the state of humanity. As he spoke, I realised that sin was my basic problem. He went on to speak of Jesus Christ in a way which I had come to associate with Christians - it was clear that there was some personal relationship involved rather than the use of a name belonging to someone who had lived a long time ago. For the first time, that evening I heard the Gospel clearly presented, and I recognised that it demanded a response.

I was simply not ready, however, to make that response. I made the excuse that I would not believe in a God who would condemn an innocent Muslim. I had known a number of every fine Muslims when I had been in the army, including King Abdullah of Jordan, and there was an element of genuine difficulty in my thinking with regard to this aspect of God's character: but I recognise now, and perhaps did so even at the time, that the basic objection that I had was not an intellectual one but rather an objection to committing myself to the Gospel.

Leith Samuel, very wisely, did not argue. I remember him saying in reply to my question and objection, 'Can the Judge of all the earth do wrong?' I really had no answer to that! He then went on to challenge me to read John's Gospel with an open mind. He guided me away from my intellectual difficulties and asked me to consider Christ. I agreed, not thinking that the reading of John's Gospel would do any good - or indeed any harm either! I agreed to read on the condition that if I were convinced that Jesus was indeed God who had died for me and my sin then I would do something about it. In turn Leith promised to pray for me.

As promised, I read a chapter or so of that Gospel each night before going to bed. A few nights later I came to John Chapter 15, and as I read verse 22 the words seemed to come out and hit me. I was reading in the Authorized Version and the first part of the verse, 'Had I not come and spoken unto them, then had they not had sin', seemed very clearly to speak to me with regard to my objections about the Muslims. But what really came home to me was the second half of that verse, 'but now they have no cloak for their sin', which I read as, 'Now you have no excuse for your sin!' I knew that was true, but still I was not prepared to surrender. My opinion of Christians had improved, but I was still convinced that they were 'wet' and inadequate and that their faith was really a crutch for those who could not cope with life. I turned over, expecting to be asleep within a few moments as was usual when working as a farmer.

Sleep, however, was not for me that night! For four hours I tossed and turned, not only sleepless but in agony of spirit as I recognised that I was fighting against God Himself. All I can remember are words coming back from many years previously, 'Why do you kick against the pricks, why do you kick against the pricks?' Eventually I could stand the pressure no more and just before 3 am on 26 August 1963 I said two words to the living God who was speaking to me, 'I surrender'.

I nudged my wife, thinking that she was asleep. In fact she had been praying for me throughout those four hours. Together we knelt at the bedside. I didn't know how to pray and used no words at all but God knew what was in my heart, and so when a few moments later we got back into bed I was asleep within three minutes.

The next evening I went to see Leith Samuel, who was still staying with my mother-in-law. I did not need to tell him what had happened because the change was so obvious in my face. He started to read to me from Romans Chapter 5, the first eleven verses, and even as he read the first sentence, 'Now therefore being justified by faith we have peace with God through Jesus Christ our Lord', I nearly stopped him and said that I knew exactly what was meant. What had I let myself in for? That very night I wondered when Mrs Samuel took me upstairs to say goodnight to their children. I knelt at the bedside and she started to pray. After she and both the children had prayed it was quite obvious that I was the only other person in the room and was also expected to pray. I opened my mouth and spoke out loud to God for the first time in my life. It was all very strange and disconcerting for a self-confident army officer and estate owner, but the deep joy within and the immediate change in our family relationships convinced me that I was now, at last, heading in the right direction.

Perhaps at this stage I should say something about our own children. At the time of my conversion our only son, George, was aged nine and his sister, Katrina, some eighteen months his junior. As described elsewhere both came to Christ as a result of seeing the difference in their father, and both have continued in the faith. George, having been called to the service of God, was eventually directed into teaching Religious Education and is now happily married with two children, living on the Moray coast. Katrina became an accomplished secretary and became engaged to a young Christian banker. They went through great trauma as to whether God wanted them to marry or not and at that time we were especially close. They are now in Morningside and have two children at primary school.

Fiona and Susan were both much younger and the change in the family relationship was perhaps less obvious to them. We left Straloch and moved first to West Linton and later into Edinburgh itself at a stage when the change from country to city and from small school to large was very hard on them both. Fiona has inherited many of the strong characteristics of her father, and having rebelled strongly at school and art college she travelled for some time in the Far East in company which gave us, as her parents, great concern.

We in some measure experienced the tension that is in the heart of God as we hated what she was doing and yet found love being drawn from us in direct proportion to her rejection of all that we stood for and believed. We learnt by experience the fact that when 'sin abounds' grace does so even more. We knew something of the poignancy of rejected love. What a joy it was when God met her, in Christ, through some American summer mission team members whom she had started off by disliking and despising.

Susan has become used to success. Despite the lack of one kidney and much trouble with asthma she has excelled at many sports from sub aqua to parachuting, and has made a considerable success of her chosen career as a nurse. She married Robert from New Zealand in 1987 and they are working in Edinburgh for some time before he takes her to his home country. Neither has yet come to Christ but we are learning to pray with faith, claiming the promises of the God of the covenant, confident but not presumptuous. What a relief it was to find that sort of faith rather than the tense, pressurising prayer which can so often cover any sense of love and result in a totally false situation in the family, where the children either 'make a decision' to keep the parents happy or turn away from Christ because they resent the feeling that somehow they are not as important or as loved as others because they do not conform to their parents' faith.

Mary was born two and a half years before we left Straloch, and Lucy when we had just moved to West Linton. I have described elsewhere how Mary came to simple faith at the age of three, and she has gone on steadily in her relationship with God. When she was a baby we were having problems with infant baptism and so she had been dedicated. It was a great joy to us when she decided to be baptised and joined the local church in Kincraig. She now teaches music in Lochaber. Lucy has spent much of her life at Alltnacriche near Aviemore and, being very keen on riding, dogs and outdoors she found it was a real wrench when we moved. She is at present at Inverness Technical College for a year, awaiting an opening for a course in Edinburgh of interior design, and commuting from Kincraig finds the lively church and enthusiastic group of young Christians there a real help in her Christian faith.

Truly we are so grateful for our family and can echo the words of Psalmist: 'Children are a reward (from the Lord) ... blessed is the man whose quiver is full of them'.

Chapter 2

SHEPHERDING WITH A DIFFERENCE

Only a few weeks later I was out gathering sheep.
I set off as usual at daybreak that September morning
to walk out the four-mile-long ridge before turning to
gather the sheep in Glenmore and converge with the
other eight men who were in their various places on
the handling fank.

My three collie dogs leapt madly about in their
usual misguided early morning zeal and it felt like just
another gathering day. As the sun rose slowly above
the Angus hills and bathed in its light all Perthshire
within my view, I stopped and looked. Countless times
I had walked the same ridge, had seen the same variety
of alpine plants, the same weather-worn rocks, the
same spring-fed hill burns growing into teeming rivers
as they tumbled towards the fertile Howe of
Strathmore; but for the very first time on that
particular morning I really noticed them in all their
intricate beauty. Something of the wonder and marvel
of God's creation entered my soul as I stood there
knowing so clearly the presence of Christ whom I had
so recently come to know. Words which I never even
remember hearing before came into my mind:

'Heaven above is deeper blue,
Earth around is sweeter green;
Something lives in every hue
Christless eyes have never seen.'

And I knew it was true.

Was it coincidence that at that moment my eyes picked out the form of a golden eagle perched on a rock, not fifty yards below us? Never had I been so close to an eagle. He saw the movement of the dogs at the instant and launched out into the void, so that I could see every feather of his body and his magnificent wingspan.

One of the attractions of the hills for me has been a sense of 'aloneness', very different from 'loneliness', although it includes a poignant sadness which is reflected in much of the poetry and music of the Highlands. But now I realised that no experience, no thrill is complete in isolation. Man is not designed to live alone, and can find life as it is intended to be only when sharing with someone else. When Adam sinned and broke his relationship with God, something absolutely vital in man died; but in Jesus we can recover that relationship, and on that September morning I found for myself what I have been finding constantly ever since - that the real joys of life are possible only when they are shared with Jesus Christ.

Always the hills have drawn me, and from earliest childhood there have been before me pictures of mountains - Alpine peaks rising above cotton wool clouds, the snow-covered Himalayas viewed from the heat of the Brahmaputra plains, the lowering mist of November closing down on a bleak Scottish mountain, or simply the ring of hills surrounding and towering over our home in Perthshire. It was not that hills had ever been a challenge to me. I farmed a Munro, Beinn a'Ghlo, for many years and yet, much to the horror of my climbing friends, never bothered to climb to the top.

It was no surprise when I discovered the thrill of ski-ing at a very early age. My family used to spend Christmas in Gstaad in Switzerland, and when I was three I accompanied them and began to discover the wonder and trauma of the one sport where mountains play an absolutely vital part.

It must have been in 1931 that I was allowed to follow the family up the local mountain - the Hornberg. There were of course no ski lifts in those days and so we climbed through thick powder snow on skis, fitted with skins, for three or four hours. By the time we reached the top and had our picnic lunch, one four-year-old boy was very tired and in a typical bad temper. We started down at last and like most children of that age under those circumstances, my one determined resolve was not to do as I was told but to go my own way. The result was predictable, and a few moments later a screaming boy with a torn ligament in the left knee was being hoisted on to the rucksack of Bruno Triani, our guide.

'Ve haff to ski a leetle fast to catch ze train', he said as he left instructions for the rest of the family and set off straight down the slope towards the station with me on his back. Never shall I forget that trip. Soon we could see the train approaching in the valley below and with a grunted 'Ve go a leetle faster' my carrier took the deep powder almost straight, deviating only for trees. The pain was forgotten as a terror and exhilaration took over but I was not altogether sorry when we caught the train by less than two minutes.

War clouds were gathering, however, to the north and east of the Alps, and by the time I was eleven it was clear that the days of the continental holiday were past. On our last such trip we spent a night in a hotel in Montreux that was the scene of some secret diplomatic meetings. Security was tight, and our family had tremendous fun playing at spies, leaving forged notes to trick the police. But somehow their response was no longer funny: fun was replaced by fear.

With such a background it was understandable that I was selected by the army to be one of the two British Officers to attend the first Norwegian army winter warfare course in January 1947. The course was for six weeks, including two weeks living out in tents or igloos in temperatures often below minus seventy degrees centigrade. We trained on skis with a forty-pound pack and rifle on our backs, averaging some sixty miles daily. Never have I been so fit! On one occasion twenty-four of us were in a tent with a wood stove in the middle. The guard was supposed to stoke the fire, but through exhaustion he fell asleep. We woke to find ourselves frozen solid in our sleeping-bags and unable to move. Fortunately one of the party came across, from an igloo, to find out what was going on. Did God indeed yet have a purpose for us?

Thus qualified, I was often asked to instruct in ski-ing both in the army and among my friends, so that when we moved to Perthshire after ski-ing in areas as diverse as Liechtenstein and Lebanon, St Christophe and Cyprus, it was only natural to get involved in ski instruction in Glenshee. It seemed most natural to use that talent for the glory of God after my conversion, and so in 1965 we found ourselves hosts to a Scripture Union house party for boys aged twelve to fourteen. As I experienced the relationship that this activity brought about between teachers and pupils, and found the ease with which the gospel could be communicated under those circumstances, the germ of a thought began to take root in my mind. Could an interest in the hills and in ski-ing form the basis for sharing the gospel with those who had similar interests but apparently no contact with the living God?

Just a year later, I had established contact with Bill Shannon of St Ninian's, Crieff, who was ski-ing with a small group of Christians. A young Church of England clergyman who had established British tourists in Switzerland asked some of us to meet him at St Ninian's. Twelve people met with Peter Goodwin Hudson that Saturday and caught something of a vision from God. We formed ourselves the name 'Compass Ski Club': the badge showed a compass with crossed skis and the cardinal points spelling out NEWS - the Good News of the Gospel.

From that insignificant start God took over. The record of the start of the Compass Christian Centre has been written elsewhere and the saga is still being developed in ever-expanding circles. Let it suffice to say that within a year God had provided accommodation for forty-five people close to the Glenshee slopes, all the finance to alter the building, heat, furnish and equip it, a godly man to act as warden and a large group of enthusiastic young Christians who volunteered to use their skills in teaching ski-ing and at the same time to share their faith. In 1967 Glenshee Lodge was officially opened as the first Christian outdoor centre in Scotland.

I was privileged to be one of two co-chairmen, and the memories of those early days still thrill me. Prayers seemed to be answered almost before they were uttered, and very early on God set His seal by using The Lodge to bring many young people to acknowledge Jesus as Saviour and Lord and show the reality of their decision by continuing to serve God and His Church until this day.

One of the outstanding features has been the group of people, both members and associates, who have faithfully supported the work with their prayers and action, and it has often been the love demonstrated by these Christians which has challenged the guests to examine their relationship with the Lord Jesus.

As God prospered the work of Glenshee Lodge, so another Christian outdoor centre was being established at Nethy Bridge, catering for those wishing to take part in outdoor pursuits in the Cairngorm area.

Eventually Abernethy developed into a fully-fledged Christian outdoor centre, providing facilities and instruction at least as good as any in secular circles. The trust who operate this centre have acquired two other properties in Arran and in Perthshire, and for a number of years I have been privileged to teach ski-ing with them on Cairngorm.

As the Compass Centre was growing I found myself called away from farming and from Glenshee to be an evangelist, and was eventually appointed by the Church of Scotland. Moves to West Linton and then to Edinburgh curtailed the ski-ing to some extent, but I still kept an active interest in Glenshee, and so it was natural that I should be involved when a large sum was gifted to the Church of Scotland for the purpose of starting a centre in the Badenoch area. For many months we searched the valley for suitable premises, but every door seemed to be firmly closed. At least it was decided to erect a purpose-built centre at Kincraig, and architects were commissioned. Their plan was costed, some fifty per cent higher than the capital available, and so almost in despair the committee asked me to design a simple building and employ someone to erect it. Designing buildings is fun but frightening. I made contact with a Christian building firm and eventually we produced plans, which were approved by the Church and a timetable was laid down. In April of that year, at a site meeting, the builder stated that he would have to order some £10,000 worth of equipment immediately if he were to keep to the schedule.

The Church was still awaiting a decision regarding a grant from the Highlands and Islands Development Board and would not give the go-ahead until that decision had been made. Together the builder and I prayed (much to the surprise of the other tradesmen present) and after prayer he simply stated: 'I believe God is behind this project. I will risk my £10,000.' Such is the faith of Abraham, inherited in Christ.

As the building was nearing completion the family and I moved to a big house just outside Aviemore, believing that God called us to work there. There were some real problems and testing times, which I will describe later, but one of the developments was that I was called to evangelise amongst skiers in Spey valley during the winter months. An anonymous donor presented a twenty-two feet long mobile caravan, which was fitted out with cartoons, literature stalls and audio-visuals and called'His Van'. For many years it occupied a position at the top of the Coire Cas car park on Cairngorm.

Many were the visitors drawn by curiosity, and always the opportunity was taken to explain the gospel in simple terms. I had large cartoons painted in oil and mounted round the walls in a sequence. The first showed a ski class with an instructor in red teaching his class the snow-plough. Everyone was paying attention, except for one pupil in green who was murmuring, 'I want to do it like that now'. The next picture showed him setting off by himself, with the instructor pleading after him and the simple caption 'My Way', as he headed for a precipice and disaster. The Bible says, 'There is a way that seems right to a man but the end of that way is death'.

In the third cartoon the pupil had knocked down four or five people in another class but rushed uncontrollably on his way shouting, 'Why don't they get out of my way?' He then lay fallen on the very brink of disaster with the cliff looming below him and just one word coming from his lips: 'Help!' The instructor had skied down and was between the fallen man and certain death, holding out his saving hand. The next cartoon showed the green-clad pupil trying to follow the instructor who was calling him to 'Follow me', but he was obviously not making anything of it until the last cartoon where he was stripped to his underpants and was about to step into the instructor's red gear which was hung on a nail with a faint shadow of a cross behind. The caption was simple - 'A new start'. What a joy it was to see a youngster go through the Parable of the Skier and see in it the truth of the Gospel. I watched as clearly she was gripped by the Gospel of the love of Jesus and gladly responded to Him with that simple faith which brings assurance of salvation.

Other opportunities opened up constantly. As we mounted the ski lift together, a member of the ski patrol asked me, 'What is God like?' I had just four minutes to tell him of Jesus. Eight years later his seeking was rewarded and he came to know God through His Son Jesus - and is now my son-in-law!

The opportunities were natural as I taught classes to ski, and it was soon clear that an official British qualification would be of help, so I took the course for instructors, operated by the British Association of Ski Instructors - and failed. What a blow to pride after forty-four years of ski-ing! All the feelings of anger and resentment that I had known at school rushed into my heart again, only to be taken away immediately by the Christ who had humbled Himself to the extent of becoming a man and going to the Cross. The difference was not due to age or maturity: it was living proof of the fact that the Spirit of Jesus truly makes a man new from inside.

Before I became a Christian I would have stalked off in a huff, but now I went on another B.A.S.I.

31

course, this time in Austria, and passed. So I have been privileged to use a natural talent to the glory of God, and have known His gracious kindness in letting me continue in a sport which has always been such a joy. Sometimes Christians feel that they have to be miserable to be doing what God requires, and of course there are times of sacrifice; but our God is a loving Heavenly Father who delights to give good gifts to His children.

Perhaps the seal was set on all of this some two years before this. I was ski-ing by myself on a day off late in the spring, and went up the tow with a man who told me he had come to Aviemore to find himself or to commit suicide. We stopped at the top of the hill and, much to the surprise of everyone else on that ski-tow, talked of Jesus for forty minutes, and a run together, and then talked more in the sunshine until I knew that there was nothing to prevent him from coming to Christ and receiving Him as Saviour and Lord by faith. I explained the sort of prayer he would have to pray and suggested he might pray as we skied down the Corie Cas. He followed in my tracks. Seldom have I skied slower; I wanted to give him plenty of time. At the bottom of the slope I turned and did not need to ask what had happed; it was clear that my friend was a new man in Christ. What a wonderful God we have!

Chapter 3

I LOOK TO THE HILLS

As a boy I had always enjoyed farming. I had 'helped' at busy times on the farm and not only had great fun but also that swell of pride which comes from being with 'real men'. Having left the army as late as thirty years of age I had a great deal to learn, but various correspondence courses during my last few months in the forces had given me some theoretical knowledge of hill farming and forestry. Besides, I was fortunate enough to inherit a real old-fashioned grieve who had been on the farm as horseman and tractor-man for sixty years since starting as a boy of twelve, and also a shepherd who had imbibed a knowledge of sheep with his mother's milk.

The learning process was not always easy. A headstrong young ex-army officer who had been used to giving orders found it difficult to accept that his ways were not always the best, and there were times when tempers flared and bitter words were spoken. Conversion to Christ had a tremendous effect on this area of my life but it brought its own problems too.

I suddenly realised that I had been cheating the tax collector for years by putting the home-heating oil into the farm accounts. When I told my auditor to amend the figures and make reparation for past years, he was utterly horrified. 'You can't do that!' he spluttered over the phone. 'The whole account will go into loss and the bank will probably reduce overdraft facilities'.

With outward certainty, but inward trepidation, I insisted on his going ahead, and was amused at his astonishment when the profit that year was exactly the figure he had suggested would be the loss. The Bible contains God's promise that 'those who honour Me, I will honour' and I was beginning to learn that God's Word is to be trusted.

The auditor was not the only one who failed to understand my new spiritual direction. As the manager of our neighbouring estate, I had occasion to order for it a new lorry. The garage apologised profusely for not being able to give a discount on commercial vehicles, but we fixed the deal, and the vehicle was duly delivered. Ten days later the garage proprietor appeared at my house with four new tyres for my own pick-up truck. When I pointed out that I had not ordered these, he smiled and indicated that the lorry deal had been a good one for him.

'But', I said 'that was for Glenfernate Estate, and you suggest that I should accept these for myself'.

'Yes of course...' and to this day I think he fails to understand why I was so adamant in my refusal. Inevitably the Christian who operates in the world of business and commerce will come up against situations where his Spirit-enlightened conscience will cause him to act in ways that are incomprehensible to his colleagues. Often the pressure is to conform because 'everyone else is doing it' and that it has become the accepted course of action is almost overwhelming. But God knows.

I realise that this might give a very negative impression of the Christian faith; undoubtedly a refusal to go along the way of the world may look as if it is a giving up of what is enjoyable. Having been a very heavy drinker I knew that I had to stop alcohol altogether, but the reaction of my shepherds was surprising: their one desire at the next ram sale was to get me drunk. Was it perhaps that they would feel better if they could bring me down to their level in this respect? How twisted can human nature get? And yet just a few weeks previously I would have done exactly the same and joined in with the general idea that a drunken spree was a great night out even though the result was to feel rotten the next day, to have a mouth like the bottom of a parrot's cage, and blush at the thought of some of the things that I had said in my drunken state.

The Gospel of Christ takes away guilt, regret and all that spoils; it sets a man free to enjoy life, without artificial stimulation. I remember the day of the calf sale early in October, a few weeks after my conversion. Every year, that day was one to try a man's temper to the very limit, and that particular year was worse than ever. One of the lorries collecting the calves was late; the car in which my grieve and three helpers were travelling broke down; one lorry had a partition loose; and the stots and heifers all got mixed up. To cap it all, in the midst of a thousand newly-speaned calves bawling their heads off for their mothers, the fence between my pens and my neighbour's collapsed in a heap. I'm told that the auctioneer was seen going around saying: 'Where's Captain Anderson? I've got to keep out of his way'. I'm also told that I spent that day quite peaceably with a grin on my face. When I got home that night my shepherd's wife looked at me somewhat strangely. 'Now we know there is something real', she said. 'We all just said, wait until the calf sale and then you'll see his temper!'

It was this same family who taught me much about human nature and relationships. Sandy was very fond of his wife and many an evening did we share together as we talked of sheep. Like so many who spend much of their time in the hills amongst dependent beasts, he had a quiet and gentle streak in him and this showed clearly in his relationship with his wife. But on the busy days of clipping or dipping, when neighbours flocked in to help and there were as many as twenty-five people sitting down to dinner, he treated her quite differently, deliberately shouting at her as if she were a slave. Is it, I wonder, a particularly Scottish characteristic to show off before other men by demeaning your wife, or is that character trait built into our fallen human nature?

That fallen human nature had shown itself in slightly different guise in my own case. I had every advantage of a loving family. My father, born in 1875, was a true product of his age and I stood in considerable awe of him. Indeed, I was scared stiff of causing him any offence and called him 'Sir' until the day of his death; and yet I loved him and kissed him goodnight every night of his life. We had that relationship with each other which meant that I could sometimes be cheeky to him and pull his leg even whilst maintaining a fearful respect. He would pretend to be annoyed, but the twinkle in his eye showed his pleasure. Partly as a result of that, I find it easier than many to know what it means to fear God as well as to love him.

My mother was a saint, although scarcely recognised or appreciated by four headstrong children. She had lost two brothers in the First War, and my own brother's death as a pilot in 1943 deepened her sadness, and I'm sure hastened her death from angina; but there was always a quiet serenity about her which drew all sorts of people to her side, simply to share her presence. She was universally loved and respected. Her Christian faith was not often expressed in words, but looking back I can see so clearly the Spirit of Jesus in every aspect in her life. My eldest sister and brother were very close indeed and my other sister was self-possessed, so I spent a solitary childhood, using a very vivid imagination to live in what was partly a world of fantasy. Love, therefore, was a difficult word for me. I felt the emotion very deeply and would often be moved to tears which embarrassed me considerably, but I knew that there was something beyond the emotion. I longed for the reality, but could find it neither in the world of fantasy nor in the real world of school, where I was taught that Christianity was an ethical system and we developed that independent spirit which called for a stiff upper lip under all circumstances. I was struck by the words of the Bible: 'Love is patient, love is kind. It does not envy, it does not boast, it is not proud. It is not rude, it is not self seeking, it is not easily angered, it keeps no record of wrongs': but they were only words.

No wonder I became involved in an emotional way

with all sorts of girls as soon as I left the monastic establishment of school. The search for love led to the girl met on VE day at Oxford; the young policeman's daughter at Barnard Castle; the sophisticated young lady at Kitzbuhl on holiday with a mother desperate to see her off (especially to an eligible young cavalry officer); the lonely YWCA worker in Luneburg. They were all attractive - but was it love? Time proved it was not. But there was something different about Joy. She had holidayed for years as our neighbour in Scotland, and my father and her grandfather had worked together in India many years before. I took her to some of the post-war Highland Balls, and the uniform and the special Alvis car undoubtedly impressed her; but there was more to our relationship than that, and I spent much time trying to analyze both thoughts and feelings. Eventually we married, and outwardly a perfectly matched couple set out on the honeymoon of life. But did I love her? Was I capable of love? What was love?

Gradually we settled into a relationship and children were born to us. I was proud of them and loved them in a rather selfish way, but my army career and later my farming life took precedence, so that the family became something for which I would work and worry but were somehow distant and remote. The relationship between Joy and myself also changed subtly over the years and the area where this was most obvious was in the spiritual. Knowing that she had that spiritual life which was denied me I felt inferior and therefore closed myself off into a world of my own. Inevitably someone else broke into that world, and the family, although outwardly retaining its appearance of success and respectability, lay on the brink of disaster. My wife forgave, and in over twenty five years has never once indicated that she has not completely erased the events from her mind. Shades of the forgiveness of God, worked out in the agony of Calvary!

Was that what drew me to Christ? Certainly it played its part, and conversion brought the certainty not only of God's forgiveness but His promise of a new Spirit: and the reality of life confirmed that truth so that others took note of the change.

Our two oldest children George and Katrina were nine and eight at the time of my conversion, and within months they had both professed their saving faith in Jesus Christ. When asked what had caused him to believe, George casually replied that he and his sister had seen such a difference in their Dad that they had decided they had better do something about it too.

Of course it was not all immediately perfect - God still had and has a great deal to do in my life and there are terrible memories of letting Him down. I remember moving black-faced hoggs from one field to another in the early spring. One was weak in body and thrawn in spirit and refused to move with the others. As I approached, it merely lay down until my patience snapped and I picked it up, beat it and threw it away in disgusted anger. A voice from across the river still rings in my ears: 'You call yourself a Christian and do that!'

Our family is by no means perfect, and still I find communication a real difficulty, but there is a new dimension since Christ came in as our Head. He is the Good Shepherd and we are His often wayward and deliberately awkward sheep. What lessons there are to be learned from those despised animals! Surely it is significant that both Moses and David had their early training amongst them.

I remember reading the tenth chapter of John's Gospel at the lambing time one year and seeing the reality of Jesus' words: 'He calls his own sheep by name....they know his voice but they will never follow a stranger: in fact they will run away from him'. I was lambing three hundred Glenfernate gimmers in the big park below the road and went round them five or six times every day with my blue bitch called Fern. They would never move as we passed: just a glance and then back to grazing, cudding or sleeping. That morning I took a different dog and allowed a young visitor to accompany me - but never again! Immediately they saw the stranger the sheep were off to the far end of the park in panic, and many a lamb I had to mother that day. Those sheep had come to trust me and my dog even as I had come to trust Jesus, but a stranger sent them racing away in fear.

Fern taught me something of trust too. She was the best all-round working collie I ever had. Unlike the sleek participants in 'One Man And His Dog', she scarcely needed a command and worked best at long range.

One gathering day I noticed that six or eight ewes and lambs had hidden in the rocks and were now breaking back, making out the hill again at a steady pace. The blue bitch saw them too although they must have been over a mile away and needed only a nod from me to set off wide to her right. The sheep stood for a moment on the top of what we call the Round Hill, and every shepherd at the gathering saw them. Mostly they pretend not to notice in case one of them was the one guilty of missing them. One or two who were furthest away shouted, with a certain smugness, 'You're leaving!' but no-one offered to do anything about it. To fire a dog at that range and in the full public gaze was to invite failure and ridicule.

The sheep strung out once more over the hill. They were soon out of sight and I have to admit to a moment of uncertainty; I had no idea where Fern was. But I trusted her and went on driving the bulk into the fank. As we were getting the last of the lambs through the gate I saw Fern and my heart swelled with pride, although it had nothing to do with me. There she was, still a mile behind, quietly bringing the awkward ewes and lambs down the track to the fank. It is that sort of trust that makes a relationship something really special. That is what Jesus speaks of when He says: 'You believe in God; believe also in Me'.

I was handling a lot of sheep at the time and needed a third dog. My black bitch Judy was great on the hill but far too wide for a lambing, and Fern was getting too old to do all six weeks by herself. Her half-sister was whiter, and most people reckon that a white dog is no use for work, so my shepherd's wife had decided to keep her for a pet, and call her Candy.

It was soon obvious that, white or not, she had all the necessary qualities in her. Never a real hill dog and not of much use on bulk, she had one of the strongest 'eyes' I have known. Once transfixed by that powerful eye, the most awkward and bolshie-minded black-faced ewe would walk quietly as directed and never dare to break or even move out of line.

God spoke to His people of old: 'I will guide you with Mine eye'. Just as the dog could never use force, as any attempt to rush in and drive the sheep in the required direction would simply cause them to break and scatter, so God knows that any attempt to force His will, His law, on human beings will result in their breaking away from him. 'Law came, sin revived and I died' is how Paul put it, and all of us know how a notice saying 'Keep off the grass' simply encourages us to walk across it.

The dog uses its eye and induces a desire in the sheep to obey. God uses His love, demonstrated by His bearing our sin and dying in our place on the Cross, to arouse in us a desire to love Him and show that love in glad obedience: 'We love Him because He first loved us; this is love for God that we keep His commandments'. The strange thing about human beings is that like dogs we so often turn away from and indeed hurt the One we love and who loves us.

'Fly' they called her, a black and white collie bitch with a mind of her own. I needed a dog in hurry for a lambing and brought her at five years old. She took a while to transfer her affection and loyalty, but once she did I could do no wrong as far as she was concerned. This was before I became a Christian. Often she was treated harshly and yet she never complained or gave up. If ever a man received undeserved love, I was that man.

One day she jumped a loose wire fence and caught her paw between the two top wires which twisted and held her in a vice-like grip. She screamed with pain, and then as I ran to her aid, and released the pressure on the wire, she sank her teeth deep into my arm.

How often people react in exactly the same way if they are frightened or out of their depth, and usually the target is a loved one. When Jesus came into the world with His frighteningly simple Gospel of a relationship with a supernatural Father God, man reacted in just the same way. 'He came to His own and His own received Him not....and they crucified Him'. His love had hardened their attitude of hostility and in hatred and fear they hit out at the One who loved them.

I went on with the rescue operation, and when it was finished Fly was all over me as if to apologise for her lapse. Jesus went on with His rescue operation even although He was losing not merely drops of blood from His arm but the life blood from His heart of love.

Perhaps it is the same sort of fear that causes many folk to resist the love of God, or perhaps it is simply because they have never seen the depth of that love which took Jesus to die at Calvary for our sin. I remember an illustration of that love involving a St Bernard dog.

Most people picture St Bernards with a keg of brandy round their necks. That is an advertising lie because, of course, alcohol being a depressant which dilates the arteries, is the worst thing you can give to anyone suffering from hypothermia. St Bernards were trained to find those overcome by the cold and then lie on top of them to keep them warm until human help arrived.

One day a Swiss farmer heard that his father, who lived in neighbouring valley, was dying. His neighbours tried to prevent him from setting out across the high pass, but the man was determined. 'I must go', he said. Two hours later, as he approached the highest point, the storm broke. Battling against the elements, cold and altitude, he was driven to his knees in delirium. He looked up and saw what he thought was a bear coming towards him. With his last strength he drew his knife and stabbed the creature three, four, five times. With its final breath the great St Bernard carefully lay on the man's recumbent body and died. In the morning the villagers found the man. He was alive. The dog's pelt and body had been enough. Jesus gave His life to keep us from spiritual death. 'He himself bore our sins in His body on the tree that we might die to sin and live to righteousness'.

The idea of giving His life followed almost immediately after Jesus had been talking about being the Good Shepherd, and one dramatic incident in my farming days brings the two very close together - the good shepherd giving his life for the sheep.

Jimmy herded at the Daldhu, eight miles from the main road. It was often cut off in the winter, but he and his family were normally well prepared. His hirsel carried about twelve hundred ewes in the spring and summer, and that March they were all high up enjoying the moss crop before the lambing was due. It started as an ordinary spring snowstorm but in the middle of the night the wind changed and the wet snow pounded down and heaped itself into fearful drifts. Hill sheep will always find suitable shelter in a storm but a change of wind at night means that their shelter becomes a trap. It took two of us with tractor-mounted snowploughs almost three days to reach the Daldhu, and when we arrived there was no sign of the shepherd.

'He's been away since the storm,' said his wife 'and I have no idea where he is'.

We knew where the ewes were likely to be-up by the Fealar march, so we walked the remaining four miles as quickly as the snow would allow. We came round the hip of the brae at last and there we saw them - eight or nine hundred ewes gathered together on a heathery slope above a deep burn filled with drifted snow. Jimmy was still digging, his hands red raw and bleeding and his whole body showing the ravages of three days without food or sleep.

Tears were running down his cheeks.

'There's still ninety-two in the burn,' he said and his strength finally gave out as he collapsed exhausted. 'I am the Good Shepherd', said Jesus, 'The Good Shepherd lays down His life for the sheep'.

As the depth of the meaning of Calvary became clearer, I began to realise that I was called to proclaim that Gospel of God's saving love and truth, and increasingly became involved in sharing my faith and preaching. It became apparent that the call of God to preach the Good News could not be combined in my life with full-time farming - there simply were not enough hours in the day.

I had another problem too. My farming system

really needed to change if it were to remain profitable; but such a change would involve sacking the elderly grieve who had taught me all I knew, and who at the age of seventy-eight lived only for his work, although he was really only capable of doing half a day. To sack him, I knew, would be to sign his death warrant.

It was at this stage that I was asked to be an assistant missioner at Edinburgh University Christian Union Mission, due to be led by Rev. Michael Green. I told the committee who approached me that I was very busy farming and had only two possible qualifications: one was an ability to do with five hours sleep or less and the other a limitless capacity for coffee. They promised to keep me busy and to supply the coffee. In the event I never had my five hours sleep any night that week and my record was seventeen mugs of coffee.

During the week I was asked to speak to the class of agricultural economists on hill farming and forestry, and in the course of my lecture I posed the problem of my grieve. The young Yorkshire lecturer and the majority of the class were quite adamant that the proper developing of the farm was the only thing that counted. At the same time, however, I noticed that the Professor and a few, just a few, of the class were not quite so dogmatic and accepted the possibility of other criteria. To them profit was not the only consideration.

My task at that Mission was not only to preach at lunchtime sessions in the King's Buildings but to be present at informal coffee evenings in the hall of residence where I was staying. On the night of the seventeen mugs of coffee, I noticed that one post-graduate law student stayed throughout. He did not often speak, but when he did it was clear that he had a brilliant and incisive mind which could make rings round my arguments. Eventually, at almost 3 am, he looked me straight in the eye and said, 'You know, what you have been telling me is that you cannot live a Christian life without Christ'. Wholeheartedly I agreed, whereupon he stood up, shook hands and left. It was not until eighteen months later he sent me a message to say that he had become a Christian.

As such conversations took place it became clear that God was telling me that this was the task for which He had called me. I knew the thrill of witnessing for Jesus, and realised that my abilities had never truly been stretched until that time. I vividly remember discussing the call with Michael Green in my car, parked on the Meadows in Edinburgh at three o'clock in the morning of the last day of the mission. I asked him how with all his intellectual ability (he had a double-first degree in Greats at Oxford and then moved across to Cambridge for two more) he could accept the Bible as completely true. His answer has remained with me ever since.

'Just two reasons', he said. 'Firstly Jesus accepted its full authority. "It is written" was enough for Him; He is my Lord and so it is enough for me'.

'And the second reason?' I asked.

'Why', he replied, 'it works!'

I went back to feeding cattle and tending sheep, and within a week received a letter from my bank manager asking me to call to discuss the farm overdraft. Not often perhaps are bank managers so used to confirm the call of God!

Within weeks I had purchased a cottage with a garden for the grieve, who was happy to give up as long as I was doing the same. I let it be known that God was calling me to be an evangelist and we arranged for the estate to be put on the market. The future uncertain - but exciting.

Chapter 4

BEGINNINGS AND BATTLINGS

Within months of deciding to leave the farm and Estate of Straloch I found myself seated at a desk in what had been the vestry of an old Edinburgh church. The room was dark and dingy, the atmosphere lonely, cold and damp, and Satan was whispering in my ear a whisper that grew into a great crescendo: 'You fool! What do you think you are doing here? Get back to a farm where you can be of some use'. Seldom have I been so close to giving up. The pressure was tremendous.

From the moment of decision about our future, we had felt almost as if we were being carried along by a powerful stream. The estate was sold without any of the problems anticipated. Arrangements were made for my replacement as Manager of the neighbouring estate, and much more importantly the Church of Scotland invited me to act as the organiser of Evangelism in conjunction with an inter-denominational movement called 'Work and Witness'. This lay movement for Evangelism had been founded a few years before by Dr D.P.Thomson. It had been this movement which had made the initial approach to me, but ultimately I was summoned before a selection committee of the Home Board of the Church of Scotland.

Perhaps the conduct of that meeting was indicative of the thinking of the Church's establishment at the time. When they heard that I had been educated at Trinity College, Glenalmond, there was a look of considerable satisfaction - Captain of the school, Trinity College, Oxford, The Royal Scots Greys (The Household Cavalry of Scotland) - ADC to a Commander-in-chief, Laird of Straloch and farming twenty-five thousand acres! At this stage satisfaction increased and fewer questions were asked. One member expressed concern at my obvious acceptance of the Bible as the completely authoritative Word of God, but this was the only mention of any subject related to the spiritual. Verily God moved in mysterious ways!

A few months later I reported to the secretary of the Home Board and only just remembered not to salute as I approached his desk. Dr Horace Walker was an older man with a very different theological stance from my own, but whose counsel and friendship I was increasingly to appreciate over the years. We seldom agreed on all points; and often, I am sure, he was deeply worried and at times mystified by what was going on, especially when he had to bear the brunt of the rage of incensed Churchmen who had so resented the shattering of their cherished, unspiritual tradition. Our opening interview was typical of his whole approach. 'We don't appoint men to new posts and then tell them exactly what to do', he said. 'Come back in six months time and tell me what God is doing and how you are getting on'.

What freedom! A 'carte blanche' for Evangelism throughout Scotland! But equally, what a responsibility! Not a guideline in sight!

My headquarters were an old church building in Fountainhall Road, Edinburgh, purchased by D.P. Thomson with a view to establishing it and many others as centres on training and evangelism, after the pattern of the St Ninian's establishment in Crieff. When I arrived it was semi-converted into accommodation of a very primitive nature, with a hall and typical old-fashioned church kitchen. A student was acting as caretaker. I had not shared in the original vision, and very, very soon found a basic principle that one leader's vision cannot be transferred to another. 'D.P.' had a distinctly individual ministry, which is perhaps one of the marks of those called to evangelism. One of my first forays with him was on a tour of the major centres of Scotland. He would assemble numbers of ministers and address them for almost an hour on 'Re-appraisal For Mission', his latest plan for organising a missionary parish. In the midst of his oratory he would suddenly stop and announce: 'And now Stephen Anderson', and sit down!

I found that I simply could not follow that, but there was more to it than the difficulties of picking up where he had left off in full flow. 'D.P.' had gathered around him a magnificent group who were loyal to him and his methods. Inevitably any change of personality or procedure would break the relationship which had been built up. The successor to any dynamic leader will always find the same as I did when I took over the management of Glenfernate. My predecessor assumed immediately a far greater respect in retrospect than he had ever enjoyed during his active

51

period. I know too that after I left I could do no wrong, although that had not been the case when I was still there.

And so I resolved that I would have to carve out a name and a role for myself. I had tried to encourage lay training at St Ninian's, Edinburgh, but the most carefully constructed courses met with little or no response. My first letter to one hundred and fifteen local ministers drew eleven replies, five or six of them negative. It was a time of apathy and an increasing antagonism to evangelism. The euphoria of 'Tell Scotland' and Billy Graham had died down and the pendulum had started its reverse swing. Billy Graham and Crusade Evangelism were bearing the brunt of the criticism but 'D. P.' too had made many enemies by his directness and unconventional approach, so that the very word 'evangelism' had acquired a dubious label and was often associated with the cults that were just starting to exert considerable influence upon young people.

Tension between the established Church and the concept of evangelism increased. Evangelism was equated with proselytism and seen as the whittling away of stalwart members of the Kirk into other Churches, or alternatively as something weird and frightening associated with rebellious youth and strange religious organisations. Many staid churches had seen those spiritually challenged by the events of the late 1950's leave their ranks to worship in what they had discovered to be the new way of the Spirit.

Most ministers, some basically insecure, saw this as a threat and drew back in anger. Only a few saw it as an example of God's judgement upon their own Church and fellowship and sought to make the necessary changes. As the lay evangelist, I posed a double threat. The threat of disturbance of the status quo was bad enough: I well remember being exhorted not to the 'rock the boat', to which I replied, 'If the boat is going somewhere rocking it may cause it harm, whereas if it is becalmed a rocking may start something!' But the threat of a layman without formal theological training, a university degree or presbyterial ordination made those who relied upon such things highly apprehensive and suspicious.

It is perhaps significant that it took nine years before the Church of Scotland found a place for my name in the yearbook. This was the day when Professor Henderson could write 'Power without Glory' and find that his powerful indictment of an established Church which relied upon its influence and power as an organisation was almost universally rejected. Many paid lip service to his ideas, but at all times his strictures against the establishment were seen as criticism of '121' or some other nebulous grouping, so his ideas were never personally applied. The Church had settled into a declining rut; but it still had the resources to maintain the ordinances of religion throughout the land, and so failed to see its need to die and be reborn. I refer especially, of course, to the Church of Scotland but the same situation was obvious in Roman Catholic and Episcopal circles, whilst non-conformist Evangelical Churches often looked on with complacent and critical pride.

The other threat to established religion at this time

came from young people. The 'Jesus Movement' had wafted across the Atlantic and brought with it both the fresh breeze of the Spirit and a host of fringe activities and organisations, many of which were later to prove spurious if not positively evil. The Church had failed to win or to keep the younger generation through 'nurture evangelism', and were apprehensive of anything else. This attitude was easy to understand. I remember, for instance, being asked to 'rescue' an eighteen-year-old girl from 'the Children of God' in Portobello. I took a young Christian girl with me and we met with the group. As we spoke, it became increasingly difficult to distinguish what, if anything, was wrong. All that was said seemed to be in accordance with Scripture, and there was such an atmosphere of love and caring in that house which was so sadly lacking in many churches that I could well understand why the eighteen-year-old had been attracted. After two hours together I suggested that we prayed and it was only then, as the leader led in prayer and the group joined in with a syncopatic chorus, that I knew that this was not of the Spirit of Jesus.

To most of the Church at that time all that was going on in the ferment of youth was frightening and to be discouraged. Displays of emotion and claims of miracles were equally disturbing to a douce Scot, so the generation gap widened and nowhere further than in the Church.

By most of the groups I visited in my early years I was associated with the lunatic fringe, and the tension within myself mounted as I sought to discern and follow the path of the Spirit of Jesus. One of the encouraging finds at that time was that wherever I travelled in Scotland there was always some signs of spiritual life. There was only one presbytery where I did not recognise a glimmer of response. Next day, however, I received a telephone call from a minister who asked me to lead a weekend with the session of his church. 'I was in presbytery last night,' he said, 'but you would not have seen me. I was behind a pillar'.

But what of the miraculous? Clearly I had experienced God working in miraculous ways in my own life and in the lives of others, but now there seemed to be an increase of the *dramatically* miraculous, and many claims were being made which caused others to feel inferior and insecure. The tension was in the Church and in myself.

One day I was due to pass by Alloa when there was a Charismatic conference being held at Gean House, and I had agreed to call in for a short time. One of those attending that conference came to St Ninians's in Edinburgh on the following day and joined our morning fellowship. This group had kept me sane during those first months and I was greatly in debt to its leader Bill Wardrop, who had so faithfully served Work and Witness at St Ninian's over the years. That morning a missionary from Aden was present and spoke of how he was due to have an operation for an ulcer within two days, but that he was convinced God wanted him back in Aden to hand over to a local Christian before the final evacuation of all Europeans. He asked us to pray for his healing, in terms of James Chapter 5. We decided that this would be right only if we had some oil, and those present turned to me. I knew of none within the building but on investigation I discovered some and so joyfully but reverently we anointed the missionary concerned and prayed, but with no apparent effect. On the Tuesday he reported to the hospital and the surgeon ordered a confirmatory x-ray, then another and another. Eventually he turned to the missionary and told him that his ulcer had completely disappeared and that he could travel to Aden as soon as he liked. The sovereign God had acted.

Such experiences, and others connected with the occult, which will feature later, could easily have diverted me from the call to evangelism, but God by His grace always kept salvation from sin as the top priority.

I had been asked to take a series of services in the Wirral and to speak at a men's breakfast there on a certain Monday morning. On the previous Sunday evening, I had been sharing Christ at a home fellowship in West Linton, to where we had moved from Straloch. A young man, married to a Christian girl who was our neighbour's daughter, was clearly close to commitment but fighting against the drawing power of the Spirit. He had been involved in the occult. I left at 10.30 pm to drive South and promised that I would pray for him on arrival. It was soon after 3.00 am when I settled to sleep in the back of my estate car in Upton St Mary, and I prayed there that God would show His victory in the life of that young man.

When I returned to West Linton towards the end of that last week, my neighbour telephoned. 'Was it soon after 3.00 am that you arrived?' he asked. On hearing my reply he said, 'I thought so', and put the receiver down! That evening his son-in-law shared his nightmare of that morning when a dark figure had chased him relentlessly in his sleep until eventually he had cried out to Jesus and awoke, just after 3.00 am, to commit his life to Christ.

I had been appointed as organiser of lay evangelism but found that people simply did not want to be organised, especially into evangelism! The events of those first few months confirmed my call not to be an organiser but an evangelist, and eventually the difference was recognised and I was officially known as the Lay Evangelist of the Church of Scotland. Today the situation is radically changed in the Church throughout the land, and the climate is right for the appointment of regional organisers of evangelism; but I trust that this distinction between the two is never lost, and that we do not merely recognise those called to organise and encourage the Church to witness but also those called to use the God-given gift of being an evangelist.

But what does this gift of being an evangelist mean in the 20th century? Is he inevitably a crusade evangelist, complete with entourage? Is he one who travels from one congregation to another? Is he someone called to exercise the gift within one fellowship and sometimes work out from that base? Perhaps none of us have really thought through some of these issues and I do not pretend to have all the answers even after eighteen years as a travelling evangelist. Nevertheless in those early days God showed me certain patterns and principles through my personal experience. He started with the experience of a 'mission' at the invitation of the kirk session of a church set in a housing estate in one of the deprived areas of the West of Scotland. It was to be a mission that influenced my whole life and ministry.

Chapter 5

EVANGELISM IS A RISKY BUSINESS

A team of twelve people gathered in Uddingston that early spring. They varied from a retired teacher of the deaf to a seventeen-year-old school leaver and included a girl in a wheelchair and an ex-racing driver. The last mentioned had not long assumed the leadership of an evangelistic youth organisation in Edinburgh that was making an impact upon the roughest of local youths but was also getting a reputation of being on the extreme lunatic fringe of the Church.

The housing area we covered was typical of many in that district at the time, with council houses in serried ranks and no amenities within reasonable distance. The tone had gone right down until any unoccupied house not fully boarded up rapidly became a wreck, while scarcely one garden survived in the whole scheme. The streets were covered in litter and roamed by two gangs, the older of which, 'The Mad Squad', was led by one Johnny Wilson who at the age of eighteen boasted thirty-one convictions. This gang even had two murders registered against them in local police files.

The church, with its adjoining manse, had been built at the same time as the scheme. Outwardly it resembled a prison with all the barricades up, but inside it was a most attractive building with excellent facilities. The minister had moved from a small

Ayrshire town where he had seen God at work amongst young people; he hoped to be likewise used to stimulate his new congregation, who had settled into an acquiescent acceptance of the miserable situation and a virtual despair for the future. Many of the elders and the missionary assistant saw the mission merely as an opportunity to get more of the 'nice' people still living in the area to join the church and swell congregational numbers, organisations and finance.

The Mission team programme was fairly traditional - a team Bible study in the morning, followed by children's games and meetings until lunch time. Visitation took place during the afternoon and a teenage cafe was held at night. Before long it became clear that God was moving in two main areas. Firstly in visitation we came across many hungry souls in the twenty-to-twenty-five-year-old age group; they had no church background whatsoever, so that no prior knowledge of the Bible or the Christian faith could be assumed. Those converted from this group were formed into small groups to study and pray together; one of the significant features was the number of songs and poems written by those among them who had come to faith in Christ.

The other area was that of the teenage cafe, and here the spiritual warfare really raged throughout the twelve days of the mission. The two gangs in the area decided that the church hall made an excellent meeting ground, and at the start of every evening fights developed. Eventually we persuaded everyone to leave razors or broken bottles at the door; the nature of the fights changed, but still there was not one night when I did not have to take at least one casualty to hospital in my vehicle. The only times the two gangs got together was to defraud the team or to steal from the shop which we set up on a trolley. Their speed at putting out lights, and in the few moments of resultant darkness and chaos stripping the tuckshop of every single item, had to be seen to be believed. Only the spastic girl in the wheelchair, or the retired teacher with a tennis racket, had any preventative effect.

Although weapons were banned inside the hall, table tennis bats and coat-hooks were sometimes used as substitute armoury, and major confrontation usually took place just outside the side door of the church. I remember the occasion when both sides lined up while their respective champions prepared to fight with cut-throat razors. I thought the brave and right thing was to separate them, and with thoughts of 'Blessed are the peace-makers' I positioned myself between the protagonists. Two from one gang stepped forward with razors at my throat and two from the other with broken milk-bottles to my face. I decided to go to the vehicle to pray, and eventually to carry the loser off to hospital.

Nothing of the Gospel seemed to get through and our attempts at an epilogue were disastrous, with personal counselling about Christ meeting with jeers and total disbelief. We were at the end of our tether and prayed desperately.

One night we had cleared the cafe by about 10.30 when there was a tremendous noise outside and Johnny Wilson, the leader of 'The Mad Squad', drunkenly drove a stolen car into the church car park with the exhaust and a rear spring trailing on the ground and making a fearful racket. A crowd of the gang gathered as I spoke through the open driver's window of the devil who had got a grip upon his life and of Jesus who alone could set him free. Suddenly there was a shout of 'Fuzz!' and in the commotion I saw Johnny clear a ten-foot, brick wall, apparently without effort, in order to evade the approaching police car. Two hours later there was a knock on the caravanette door where I was sleeping and Johnny came in. 'I know you were right about a devil in me', he said, 'and I want to let Jesus in to change me'. Together we knelt and prayed, and then he asked me to accompany him to the house where he had stolen the car. With a raincoat over my pyjamas I did so. We walked into the house, where the lights were still on, to find the car owner, a lady, giving details to two young police officers. Johnny made his confession and asked the owner for forgiveness, promising to pay for any damage caused. Never shall I forget the expression on the faces of those two policemen.

But more was to come: I was visited by the police sergeant the next morning and as we spoke his eyes caught sight of the bunch of keys lying on my desk. He asked me where I had obtained them, because they belonged to Johnny Wilson and were known to open any normal make of car. 'He never lets them out of his sight', said the police sergeant. It was hard to convince the man that, earlier that morning, Johnny had quietly handed over those keys for me to keep.

The police sergeant was not the only one who

found it hard to believe that there was a real change in the group as one by one members of both gangs came to receive Christ as Saviour and Lord. The church people had been horrified by what had been going on in their premises, and when over fifty of the two gangs turned up for the service on Sunday morning (the only evidence of razors being shaven chins) they were naturally terrified and drew as far away as possible from this dangerous new congregation. You can imagine the effect upon the young folk.

Fifty-six of them had professed conversion and asked for a weekly Bible study and prayer meeting. The minister was overjoyed but the session refused point-blank the use of any church premises. The meeting was consequently held in the manse, and over sixty turned up on that first Wednesday. But the pressure was on, and eventually the opposition was so great that the minister was forced into hospital with a nervous breakdown.

Ten days after the mission I was called to Dr Walker's office. Without comment, he showed me a letter from that session in which complaint was made about the Home Board evangelist because certain property (and this was listed as five pieces of sports equipment, three coat hangers and one fire extinguisher) had been irreparably damaged. I looked up, and the Secretary of the Home Board quietly handed me another letter in which he had acknowledged the one from the session and noted its contents. The final paragraph read: 'the Home Board also notes with considerable satisfaction that a number of young people came to a living faith as a result of this mission'.

Did it last, or was such an experience merely the result of mixing with young people of their own age and finding some activity in a dull and drab existence? That was the big question. Was it all emotionalism which would melt like snow as the months went by? Some sadly did fall away, but perhaps the most influential factor in their cases was the unwelcoming attitude of those within the church. Some are proving the reality of the power of God by their perseverance under desperately difficult conditions. Perhaps 'Shug' is the best example of this.

Hugh Culborn was always known as Shug, and was recognised as the finest fighter for miles around. He had that truly pugnacious spirit which never lost its temper and preferred odds of three or four to one. I, who had been a boxer, recognised that I was watching a man who might well have been the light middle-weight world champion if he had been trained as a youngster. His speed and ferocity were awesome to watch. I was often the one to carry him off to hospital after he had been fighting single-handed against a group of perhaps six or seven. One night he was terribly battered and bleeding and I waited for him to be stitched up. Driving back late with some sixteen stitches in his face and bruises like over-ripe plums across his face, he turned with a somewhat sickly smile and said, 'You know, I got to thinking in that hospital - if I'm going to get beaten up it may as well be for something worthwhile. I've decided to become a Christian'. I put Shug in touch with a group of local Christians, and did not see him again for over a year. When I did so he had two front teeth missing.

'Oh, Shug', I said, 'you've been fighting again'. 'No, I haven't', he replied indignantly, 'though I was sore tempted; there were three of them came at me with sticks, just the right odds, but I never fought back'. Seldom has the injunction to turn the other cheek been taken so literally!

But was this a unique situation in a unique place, unrelated to the life of Scotland in the 1970's? Most church people would probably have thought so. It was all right for books like those about Nicky Cruz to be published and admired from a distance, but these things were only for those on the very fringe of society, and especially across the Atlantic. I remember giving details of certain incidents on mission to my uncle-in-law who was a highly respected elder, church treasurer and successful farmer. It was quite clear from his reaction that although he was too polite to say that he did not believe me, in reality he was convinced that I was exaggerating to the point of untruth. I met almost the same reaction wherever I went in Church circles, and even Horace Walker, in our long discussions, was obviously deeply puzzled to know how I, who seemed perfectly sane and logical in discussion, could possibly mean what I said about what was going on in our land. Even today there is a reluctance to recognise the truth about the degradation of our society. Is it perhaps because to admit that these things can happen on our very doorsteps is to admit that the whole of humanity is tainted by original sin, and because that thought is one which respectable people prefer to keep at a respectable distance?

There were even times when I too wondered if I were exaggerating or reading more into a situation than actually was there. For a number of years I was privileged to lead the Church of Scotland summer mission to Port Seton camp. At that time the camp consisted of wooden huts designed to sleep eight but mainly containing twenty to twenty-four people. The church and manse were central to much of the life of those on holiday. It was a small mission team but perhaps the 'glamour team' of its day, because it was very clearly in the front line of mission. Most of the families in the camp were from deprived areas and, this being the only holiday affordable, the whole family came together so that teenagers and older children formed the highest percentage age group; it was they who dominated the sundown services and sing-alongs.

It was not therefore a conventional congregation who gathered each evening, and on many occasions a service was interrupted by an outbreak of violence. I think of one very tense evening when rain had made sure that the sing-along would be held inside the church building. It was packed and tension was running high as the Glasgow and Paisley holidays had overlapped and the rival gangs were almost at boiling point. I was relieved when two local Christians joined us at the prayer meeting before that evening. Both brothers were farmers in East Lothian and built to suit! They stood solidly at the back as potential bouncers. As the service started and as a restlessness developed I called one of the brothers forward and asked him when he had become a Christian. 'When I was three', he replied in a solid East Lothian accent. 'I mind kneeling at my bedside and asking the Lord Jesus to come into my heart and He came'. You could have heard a pin drop in that church.

It was not always so restrained. I remember one occasion when the motor-cycle gang decided to race round the church at the time of the evening service. That was bad enough, but when two of them drove up the steps at full speed and into the makeshift aisle we felt it was time to call a halt. I will always remember that as the Christians stayed behind in the church to pray, an elderly solicitor from Tranent lifted up his voice to God: 'Oh, Lord, forgive us. Forgive my generation. It is our fault that these youngsters are like this'. Shades of Nehemiah who prayed, 'I confess the sins we Israelites, including myself and my father's house, have committed against You'. How we need that sense of corporate guilt in the Church if we are to see the reviving power of God!

God was undoubtedly at work both in dramatic and personal ways. One young teacher had been converted at Moray House and was a valuable team member, but she somehow lacked something of that peace and assurance which is the Christian's birthright. As I prayed with her a very clear thought came into my mind and I knew that I had to say that her father only really loved her as a success whereas her Heavenly Father loved her for herself and just as she was. In floods of tears Alex spoke of how disappointed her father had been that she had been born a girl and had not entered the family business. The unconditional love of our Heavenly Father flooded over and into her to bring a new relief and unutterable joy.

It was just a few days later she and Moira, another teacher in training, were called to a hut where three children had been deserted for the evening by their parents who were at the pub -not an uncommon occurrence. The two younger children were screaming, but for a long time their nine-year-old brother had kept the two team members out of the hut by wielding a stick, with the clear intention of doing them grievous bodily harm. At last the poor sisters were brought into the manse. They were covered, not only in lice and fleas, but with scabies. With fervent prayer, claiming the protection of Almighty God, the two teachers scrubbed and polished the two mites, dried them off by the fire and gave them a meal, which was wolfed as though they had not seen food for weeks. The love of God spread abroad in our hearts is very practical. Three hours later the parents returned and were furious, not only with the children but also with us. An hour later our two girls were still getting fleas out of each other's long hair.

Yes, God was clearly at work, but something gave me cause for grave concern. Teenagers and children professed conversion by the score and many showed an immediate hunger for the things of God; some wrote songs and poems which were truly beautiful and showed a deep grasp of the Scriptures and of the things of the Spirit. But gradually I noticed that the same youngsters were coming back year after year professing conversion every summer but giving no evidence of that conversion at home for the rest of the year. What was wrong? Was it our fault? Did we preach an emasculated Gospel? Did we not stress the need for repentance? All these thoughts raced through my mind and disturbed my spirit until unbelief began to creep in, and that cynical attitude found a foothold with the assumption that this whole mission was merely an emotional and cultural experience among easily influenced teenagers. The summer missions at Aberdeen came just after Port Seton; it was these that God used to dispel in me this cynical spirit of unbelief.

I inherited the tradition of a beach mission which in Tom Allan's day had seen five hundred gathered on the sands. The presbytery was quite certain that this was the venue, and arranged a presbytery service on the first Sunday at 3.00 pm. The beach that afternoon was as cold as Siberia and a total of thirteen people were present. As the week progressed we found ourselves in direct competition with the red-coats - an army of youth workers hired by the council to entertain children. We held our own and managed to attract a few more children than they did, but it was quite clear that God was indicating that this was not the place for a mission. We therefore moved to Hazelhead and Duthie Park, with lunch-time and evening services at St Nicholas' Kirkyard in Union Street. I do not think that the presbytery has ever forgiven me for this 'flitting', but God honoured the move. The Kirkyard was the ideal preaching station. Standing on a gravestone and singing 'Up From the Grave He Arose', or borrowing a set of bones from a passer-by and using them to illustrate a sermon from Ezekiel 36 - 'Can these bones live?' - were unforgettable experiences.

One night the evening service had just started when a commotion, indeed an uproar, started in Union Street. A man was shouting, with the high-pitched hysterical voice of one under the influence of demons. 'Don't listen, don't believe him! God is evil! Satan is good!' He had, inevitably, drawn a considerable crowd around him, and advanced purposely to where I was standing and preaching. I have always had an immense and unreasonable dread of any hysterical crowd, and my knees were knocking in terror as I retreated to the end of the microphone lead and looked around for support, only to find that the team had retreated a further twenty yards, with their backs to the wall.

I continued, however, to preach as the man advanced with red, glaring eyes and tried to seize the microphone from my hand. In terror I watched as his hand, some eighteen inches from my own, was apparently gripped by an immense and unseen force. His hand quivered but was held. Shaking with fear, my voice went deep and quiet as I continued to speak of the love and power of the crucified Christ. After ten minutes the man went quietly to a gravestone and started sobbing. The crowd were deeply silent, and a policeman came up and asked if help were required, but by that time the situation was clearly in the hands of a higher law. Later I was approached by two young Americans whose typical response was, 'Man, that was beautiful!'

It was the following year that we decided to rent

the Music Hall to promote a gospel rock concert. Much good publicity was distributed, and tickets were on sale in advance; but four days before the concert was scheduled we had sold fewer than fifty tickets for a hall seating some two thousand people. We prayed, and decided that a loudspeaker on the top of a car going around the housing estate would be a good idea, but the police insisted that we get permission from the magistrates. The clerk laughed sardonically when he heard what we intended to do. Five magistrates had to sign the forms, and it was in the middle of holiday time. I asked the clerk to complete the form, adding that we would pray and I would get in touch with him that night. When I phoned the magistrate's clerk, he was aghast. 'Five magistrates came in this afternoon; your form is signed and you can go ahead!'

Nevertheless, as we gathered on the evening of the concert, we only had one hundred tickets sold. The janitor was sympathetic but realistic, saying that we needed a good shower of rain, which might bring more in. But there was no sign of a break in the weather: it had been blazing hot for ten days and the high-pressure area was still firmly over the granite city. Almost without thinking I blurted out, 'We'll pray and it will rain'. He walked away with a superior smile.

The prayer that night was very simple and quite clear. 'Lord, we ask for a heavy shower - not enough to spoil things for holidaymakers, but enough to bring people to the concert and to show the janitor Your power, for Your Name's sake'. As we rose from prayer a team member came diving in, almost incoherent. 'It's raining!' We had some five hundred at the concert that evening.

The next day the story featured in the Press & Journal, and a few days later the matter was raised in the Aberdeen Presbytery by a minister who objected and who, it transpired, had got wet when playing golf! Another minister rose quietly in his place and quoted from James, Chapter 5, verses 17 and 19: 'Elijah was a man just like us. He prayed earnestly that it would not rain and it did not rain on the land for three-and-a-half years. Again he prayed and the heavens gave rain'.

'My God,' he said quietly, 'hasn't changed. Has yours?' He resumed his seat in silence and the presbytery moved to the next item on the agenda. Perhaps the real test of faith always lies here. Is our God the living God of the Scriptures, the God of Abraham, Isaac, Jacob, Peter, Paul and of us? Has He changed or is He indeed the same yesterday, today and forever?

But if He is the living God, then surely He shares our humanity, and that includes the gift of humour. We had been very busy that year and one of the team, an eighteen-year-old girl, was getting exhausted, but Julie was determined to keep going. Before the evening Open Air, we prayed in the cool crypt below the Church of St Nicholas. That night conversations after the meeting went on until almost midnight. When eventually I counted the team one was missing. 'Where's Julie?' No-one had seen her since the prayer meeting three and a half hours before. We dashed to the crypt, unlocked the door, and found her still on her knees - fast asleep. What a marvellous relief that laughter brought! There is a levity which is highly destructive to spiritual work but there is a lightness which can echo the humanity of Christ.

One year we had permission to park a large static caravan in the forecourt of the Langstane Kirk in Union Street. We called it 'The Fool's Paradise' and had tracts printed, giving the Bible teaching on folly and wisdom. The greatest crowd-puller was when my son, dressed in a jester's uniform, sat in silence on the crossbar of a lamp-post for twenty minutes. The crowds gathered and when I asked the question what was he doing there his reply was 'Being a fool for Christ', which introduced his presentation of the gospel. Perhaps some rejected such activities as 'antics' or 'gimmicks' and perhaps some felt that the Gospel was being demeaned; but people were being reached in the very centre of a busy city and reached not merely with a gimmick but with a prayer-watered, Biblical Gospel.

One of my greatest joys in Aberdeen was the unflinching support of an elder in the Free Church. He was regular at our meetings and seldom missing from the preaching. The culture was miles apart; our language in prayer was totally different and the music must have been a sore trial to him, but that did not matter. His one desire was to see the Gospel proclaimed and Christ exalted.

Not all are big enough to get past the prejudices and realise the realities. Rev. William Still of Gilcomston was another such character. He attended the Rock Gospel concert in the Music Hall which must have scarified his musical soul, but at the end his comment was typical of the spirit of the man. 'Stephen,' he said, 'I thought it was an awful noise - but Christ was glorified'. Paul writes, 'I have become all things to all men so that by all possible means I might save some. I do this for the sake of the Gospel...' (1 Cor. 9:22-23). Evangelism is a risky business!

Chapter 6

TRENDS AND TENSIONS

Evangelism is a risky business because it arouses the passions of unbelievers and stirs up spiritual, and therefore often physical, opposition. The devil, discounted by so many in our so-called age of enlightenment, will, like many a snake, strike only when disturbed. His ways can be violent and very obvious as in Port Seton and at Aberdeen, or more subtle as he works through lies, subterfuge and the occult.

It was in Clydebank, on a combined churches mission, that the topics on which I was due to preach were advertised in advance. One of these, scheduled for the Thursday, was on the subject of the devil. At the prayer meeting immediately before the service a young American on the team (and who now serves as a highway patrol man with the Californian police) shared with us a dream he had had in which he saw the church where the meeting was being held entered by three figures in black. They had approached the preacher, with the obvious intention of attacking him.

'What happened then?' I asked.

'I don't know', he replied. 'You see, I tried to prevent them and was killed'. You can imagine the consternation and fear as we prepared for that service.

Having made sure that the American was seated nowhere near the aisle and so would not be tempted into any heroics, I went in with my knees knocking. At

the first hymn I knew God was saying to me that Satan
was a liar from the beginning and that we need have
no fear. I recounted the dream to the congregation
and claimed the victory of Jesus. That night the
presence of God moved in power throughout the
church as the Word was preached, but at the same
time there was a tremendous sense of tension and
opposition as the Word touched those connected with
the occult. At the mention of secret societies one elder
in the Congregational Church who was high up in the
Masonic hierarchy rose in fury and stamped out of the
church, slamming the door so hard behind him that
one of the glass panels was shattered.

This type of opposition from Satan, often more
subtle, and parading under the guise of religion, was
to be my constant experience within the organisation
of the Church. Much of it seemed to stem from
Masonry, which either had a grip on men or had them
totally deceived. The prayer convener of the combined
church mission to Dumfries was an Episcopalian,
deeply committed to his church and to the mission. He
was also a very successful businessman with several
drapery shops. After one service he asked to see me,
and we spoke of Freemasonry and Christianity for
some two hours. I pointed constantly to the Scriptures
and we prayed together before he left. Two days later
he showed me his letter of resignation, which made it
clear that he had been very high in the establishment
of Masonry.

I warned him that his business was likely to suffer
if he sent that letter but he too had considered that
likelihood and was firm in his determination. Three

years later he was left with only one shop and on the verge of bankruptcy, but his joy in the Lord was a delight to behold.

Not all satanic attacks have been so repulsed in the Spirit of Jesus. Very often his target is within the Church itself to weaken the witness and destroy the unity. There is a dramatic parable that I have used on a number of occasions which makes this point.

'Ladies and gentlemen, I regret to inform you that Britain is at war. An emergency government announcement on TV and radio speaks of enemy forces landing by parachute and advancing rapidly on our major cities. The situation is of the utmost seriousness. There are two major problems. Firstly, the enemy has developed a secret weapon which kills without the victims' being aware of it. Secondly many of our forces have become so bewildered that they have unwittingly changed sides. The government warns that we are in deadly peril. There is, however, one hope: the Commander-in-Chief of our own forces has voluntarily submitted himself to the enemy's secret weapon. He has successfully come through the ordeal and is so able to provide a totally effective antidote. We are all called upon to receive and make use of this antidote freely available and to persuade our armed forces to receive it and go on to defeat the enemy'.

On one occasion this was broadcast over the camp tannoy in Port Seton and some people in Tranent, almost four miles away, telephoned the police. On another, I was at a large gathering in Aviemore and after the first sentence two army reservists ran out and reported to the local police station in order to re-enlist.

Nevertheless the point is made that Satan deceives those within the Church, and, unlike Paul, many Christians today are totally ignorant of his devices. One of his favourites is to cause dissension among believers. I soon found that in most of the non-conformist denominations it was considered practically impossible to be a Christian within the Church of Scotland, and here I rejoiced at the fact that I was appointed not only by the national Kirk but also by the inter-denominational Work and Witness movement. Within my own Church I found factions which looked on Bible-believing evangelicals with a suspicious and critical spirit. Christians - especially those in positions of leadership - seemed to walk round each other sniffing like Alsatian dogs on stiff legs. The 'label' or 'stable' seemed to take priority over the recognition of the Spirit of Jesus.

I remember being met at Wick station early in the morning by a member of another denomination. His first question was; 'What is your opinion of the Scriptures?' It was only after my reply, 'I believe in the inspiration and inerrancy of Scripture', that my hand was warmly shaken. It seemed then (and sadly the situation has not yet been fully resolved) that the shibboleths of language and jargon were more important than the command to love each other and to maintain the unity of the Spirit.

Perhaps the reasons are easy to find, but I wonder if these excuses are spiritually valid. Evangelicals were used to being on the defensive against a liberalism which had swept the Gospel away with the Bible. Tolerance and compromise were the virtues extolled in ecclesiastical circles, so that those who paid heed to the Scriptures were naturally defensive and apt to become suspicious quickly.

I was one of the first to be asked to join a small group of men within the Church of Scotland who held to the Scriptures and the primacy of expository preaching. After much heart-searching I declined because I recognised that I would have been inevitably labelled a 'Stillite', which would have restricted my possible use throughout the Church of Scotland. I was constantly being told by the Home Board and others that I should seek to take the middle ground. It was several years later that I read in John Wilson's book, 'Pity My Simplicity', the analogy of the sheep which feature so prominently in the Scriptures as the type of human beings: he pointed out that for sheep the middle of the road was a very stupid place to be and a dangerous one. I had meanwhile come to the same conclusion and had been graciously received into what has become known as 'the Crieff Brotherhood'.

This group of men has increased in number very considerably during my time as evangelist and has roused passions within the Church both for and against. Those within the group have sometimes, very hurtfully, judged and criticised other evangelicals within the Kirk, while those outside (and perhaps I detect here the faintest note of jealousy) have been heard to go so far as to say that this movement of ours is the greatest hindrance to the work of the gospel this century. I do not seek to justify either position, and see clearly faults on both sides. The brotherhood is by no means perfect - 'We see not yet all things put under subjection to Christ' as the writer to the Hebrews says - but neither are those perfect who criticize it with such venom. It is that venomous spirit which smells of sulphur and the pit and is still by no means absent.

Perhaps the rise of two parallel movements in the seventies will be seen from the perspective of history, and indeed of eternity, as being so important in the economy of God that satanic opposition through disunity was inevitable. The first was the charismatic movement, and the second was that upsurge of conservative evangelicalism which brought Bible believers in the Church of Scotland out of their defensive hiding places into the forefront of the spiritual battle and so to a dangerous limelight. The first movement brought people together under the banner of the Spirit, and in so doing caused both a unity and a disunity. The second movement brought people together under the banner of the Word, and had the same effect. When overlap occurred some of the barriers were broken down, but the pull towards disunity was extremely powerful. Satan was not going to allow the Spirit of God and the Word of God free in Scotland without a fight.

This disunity and fragmentation of God's forces came to the surface with regard to crusade evangelism. This is clearly not the place to enter into the arguments for or against such a method of evangelism - arguments which range from theological to pragmatic. Perhaps the fact that both positions - that of crusade evangelism and of nurture evangelism

- are genuinely held by Christians who draw their understanding from Scripture, and that God has blessed both approaches in practice in our day, should give us reason to suppose that the Spirit 'blows where He wills' and can use methods other than our own. The tragedy surely is when people are so entrenched in their own position that any other is seen as something to be deprecated.

When William Still gave up evangelistic rallies in Aberdeen on Saturday evenings and substituted a church prayer meeting, many evangelicals in the city spoke discouragingly of his backsliding from the evangelical faith; many others took strong objection to the possible recall of Billy Graham in the seventies: they insinuated that crusade evangelism always resulted in emotional and shallow conversions and that such activities took prayer, effort and finance away from the true long-term work of God through His Church. On a number of occasions I was caught in the middle of this debate and found myself not only torn inwardly but often rent asunder by others.

While based in Edinburgh I was invited to a luncheon given by an American evangelist who felt called to hold a city-wide mission in the capital. I met him that morning and suggested that if he were to win over Church leaders in Edinburgh he might be wise to be less flamboyant in his approach and style of dress. He disregarded my advice, and during the discussion after lunch it was clear that most of those present gently rejected his claim to have been sent by God to lead such a crusade at that time. I expressed that view on behalf of others who were present and in consequence suffered the most harsh verbal treatment on the telephone that night. I was told very clearly that I was out of God's will and that my ministry could not prosper. It was difficult not to feel either hurt or superior.

Later I had the opportunity of working with Dr Luis Palau and I remember a deeply spiritual meeting with him in the George Hotel in Perth. I pleaded with him to meet with certain Church leaders in Glasgow before undertaking his Kelvin Hall Crusade, but others advised against this. As a result, when those influential leaders found themselves unable fully to commit themselves or their congregations to the crusade, a spirit of polemic and even public mutual criticism arose. The fault was by no means all on one side: some of the statements made by fellow Christians about Luis Palau and his team and methods were less than loving and at times positively slanderous.

Perhaps an incident during the Satellite Crusade in Perth illustrates how the devil can stir up trouble but shows also how he can be defeated. The Canadian member of the Luis Palau team was preaching, and he spoke about Moses in a light-hearted, joking fashion which might have appeared as being disparaging to the Word of God.

Many of us were concerned, and it was clear that a deep division could break up the united effort until the Free Church minister, with tears in his eyes and an agony of spirit, went to rebuke the speaker. Because of his attitude the rebuke was accepted and unity maintained. Such is the victory of the Cross.

I have to admit that when I was first called to

evangelism I saw myself as a Billy Graham or a Brownlow North, with lights flashing in the big auditoria of the land! It was many years later that a young man, leading a gospel rock group working with me in the town hall of Clydebank, with a really rowdy audience of teenagers, said to me, 'Stephen, why is it that working with you we generally end up in dirty little halls with a rowdy crowd of snotty-nosed kids?' It took some time to learn the lesson that I had to be a 'failed evangelist' before I could be used of God. The glamour and publicity of my imagination had to die if Christ alone were to be exalted. In one mission the committee proposed to distribute a copy of John's Gospel, with a pamphlet 'Journey Into Life' printed at the back, into each of the 20,000 homes in the area. I was asked to write a short foreword but was horrified to find that my photograph had been inserted on the inside cover. The committee could not understand my concern, and was convinced that you had to sell the man before you could get people to come to hear the Gospel. I remembered the words of James Denney - 'No can man make much of himself and Christ at the same time'.

Combined Churches missions were taking place at that time, in Scotland, and not only those on a large scale, with imported evangelists. I think of a campaign in Motherwell called 'Jesus Alive 75' where the main events were held in the Civic Centre and included an exhibition and dramatic events in the theatre, as well as preaching in the main concert hall by the Rev. George Duncan. The problem was, as is so often the case with big evangelistic events, that the majority of those coming were already Christian - including bus loads of Lanarkshire Brethren with all the ladies in hats. The main meetings became more 'convention' than evangelism. Increasingly I saw my role as going into a community to preach where ordinary people were located.

Schools missions and open-air witness had played an important part in Motherwell. I remember two occasions in the open air. On one I was preaching opposite a new shopping centre in Brandon Parade, and very few stopped to listen. As an illustration of the free grace of God offered in the Gospel, I took out a five-pound note from my pocket, held it high and shouted over the loudspeaker that it was available for anyone who would come and receive it. A crowd of almost one thousand gathered but for eight minutes no-one came up to receive the note. Eventually a woman plucked up courage, took it and ran (probably to the bank to check its authenticity). The other occasion was outside Dalziel Church when a very talented gospel jazz band was playing. I asked if a young soprano who was on my team could sing with them. The leader looked somewhat scornfully at the girl, who was training for opera and did not look like a conventional singer. He reluctantly agreed to play 'How Great Thou Art'. From the very first note there was a sense of the presence of God, and the band played with a new sensitivity as a huge crowd gathered in awed silence listening to the song and the testimony which followed.

These experiences helped to confirm that God was calling me to concentrate outside the traditional gatherings and preach to people in the pubs, clubs and bingo halls of our towns and cities. A year or two after the Motherwell crusade, Dundee Evangelical Union invited George Duncan and myself to lead a campaign based at the Caird Hall. Three memories of real significance are worth recounting.

The first is of seeing some three hundred young people gather each evening in the Marrott Hall for a late evening rally, with a very considerable response - especially to the invitation given on the first night by Ian Leitch.

The second is of the Regent bingo hall. I went there with a small team, including the singer Barry Crompton, on the Tuesday evening. Our presentation was extremely well received, and the manager bemoaned the fact that only four hundred were present. 'If you could come back on Friday ....' I told him that I could not bring a singer but would gladly come myself that Good Friday and tell the audience about its meaning. Almost one thousand people listened to the preaching of Christ and Him crucified that night, and I have never, before or since, received such a standing ovation. Many hundreds of tracts were given out and gladly received.

My third memory is a sadder one. Some years later a group wishing to organise a city crusade in Dundee got in touch with me and indicated that the previous campaign had been a failure and that the organising group were spiritually dead. How common it is to think that God is only really active when things are being done in our way, - and how tragic! Have you noticed how often people speak of 'a great work' only when they have been involved with it?

Perhaps it was that individualistic attitude amongst evangelical Christians which had caused a coming together, under the leadership of Tom Allan in the late fifties, to fall apart after a time. Despite that, by 1972, a number of us felt bold enough to call a conference on evangelism. Detailed planning took place for over a year. Dr J I Packer was invited to lead the Bible studies. Seminars on a great variety of subjects were meticulously planned, and each day there were plenary sessions for worship, for analysis of the situation, for comment and for sharing. Part of the university of St Andrews was booked for the occasion and most societies and para-church organisations held stalls in the exhibition in St Salvator's hall.

Three significant memories stand out. At the plenary session of the first evening we attempted to provide a realistic picture of what God was doing in and through His church.

The presenter telephoned me a month before the start of the conference saying that he could find plenty of people to give success stories but not one who was prepared to be honest enough to speak of failure. Perhaps there are no failures with God? Or perhaps we somehow think that to admit failure is to let God down?

On the second evening I interviewed a young man who had been on the world 'hippy' trail. He was a confirmed user of cocaine but had been dramatically converted and delivered from drug abuse at a summer mission in Ayr. Immediately after the session I was approached by a well-known American editor suggesting that the young man should tour the USA giving his testimony. I said I would pray over this and slept on it. In the morning a wise Christian friend strongly dissuaded me. 'He will start to dwell on the past and revel in the present glamour, and his spiritual life will be ruined'. If only others with a dramatic testimony -and I think especially of Doreen Irvine the converted witch - had heeded such wise advice and had been kept out of the limelight until completely rooted and grounded in Christ - what heartaches would have been avoided.

The third memory was of going through the 'feedback' questionnaires we had asked delegates to complete before leaving St Andrews. Almost exactly half complained bitterly that the conference had been too charismatic, and the other half that it was not charismatic enough. Half complained that there was too much emphasis on the Scriptures rather than experience, and the other half that experience had featured too prominently at the expense of the Scriptures. What could we learn from such a response - that you cannot win? Perhaps. But perhaps, too, that our balance had not been very far out.

The idea of that conference had emanated from the Lausanne Conference on Evangelism, and it had been hoped that the result would be a surge of united evangelism throughout Scotland. In the event the 'National Initiative in Evangelism' which emerged from St Andrews rapidly became bogged down in establishment thinking as every denomination wanted representation and the bureaucratic wheels ground inexorably to a halt. Only an ecclesiastical committee could give birth to a name like that: such a child was bound to be either still-born or so weak as to ensure its early demise. Looking back, it was clear to see that the time was not yet right.

But the effort was by no means wasted. After fifteen years I see that conference as a turning point in Scotland, when the Kirk, having turned its back on crusade evangelism, had begun to put evangelism, Bible study and prayer back on to the agenda. There was still a long way to go before the evangelical position was to receive any real recognition but a step had been taken, and a number of congregations were now beginning to enquire how they could get involved in the spread of the Gospel. That movement was to gain momentum until evangelism became accepted within the Church of Scotland and in other denominations and began to take its rightful place on the agenda.

Chapter 7

MEANS AND METHODS OF MISSION

With the stirring of interest in evangelism amongst many congregations it was clear that a new emphasis and method were called for. God had undoubtedly used the big crusade in Scotland, and is still using this method of evangelism powerfully in other parts of the world; but a new pattern seemed to be required in our land with the emphasis on Church-based evangelism and the training of all members, or at least the committed members, to share their faith in life and word. Because this emphasis stressed what more recently has come to be called 'life-style evangelism', at the expense of verbal expression or proclamation of the truth of the Gospel, many evangelistically minded Christians were highly critical and, seeing clearly the danger of losing the sharp cutting-edge of the true Gospel, shied away from such outreach. In their thinking evangelism was restricted, on the one hand to an evangelistic method of communicating the Gospel, or way of salvation, on the other hand to a ministry of expository preaching which would bring about the re-birth. Both extremes led easily into an exclusive spirit, with one despising the other and considering that the heart of the matter had been lost. Those of the expository preaching school and the advocates of Christian character lifestyle as the vehicle of the Gospel saw the superficiality of the evangelistic Gospel. Others thought that the cutting-edge of the

Gospel had been lost in the wider teaching ministry.

Signs of this tension within evangelical Christians were evident at the Lausanne conference and the ensuing covenant document. The seeds of revolutionary, liberation theology were thrusting out aggressive shoots, and it was by no means easy to maintain the Biblical balance of the Word spoken out and the Word lived out, or the balance of righteousness and justice and submission to authority.

With the view of bringing evangelism on to the agenda of the 'normal' church in Scotland, I proposed a seven-stage period of mission, normally lasting some twelve to fifteen months. This has evolved over the years but the basic principles and phases have not changed and form, I believe, a pattern for any church which wants to get involved in long-term effective evangelism. It is of course a special effort, and as such is open to the criticism that evangelism should be a continuous process, not bursts of energy which may leave a congregation exhausted at the end.

This is at the crux of the current debate. The Church of Scotland is attempting to encourage the missionary-minded presbytery and congregation to engage in a long-term continuous strategy of evangelism: clearly this is an aim which is entirely laudable but it is likely to consider this and 'a mission' as mutually exclusive. My experience is that a short period of sharp, evangelistic effort is often required to trigger off the on-going work in any congregation. A parable illustrates the dilemma.

Once long ago in the days of whaling ships there was a big whaler with an excellent captain, good officers and a first-rate crew. One season they set off for Antarctica in good time, but found the long haul south increasingly boring. Crew members had nothing to do and spent much of the time below decks, playing dominoes and sleeping. One by one they developed a persistent disease akin to sleeping-sickness which gradually reduced their capacity to think or do any useful work.

The captain was not unduly worried. There was plenty of time. But as the days went by the situation deteriorated to such an extent that he decided to send four officers below decks to waken the crew. The infection spread, however, amongst the officers as well, until only the captain and a few loyal members were fit for duty.

At this stage the captain called a meeting of his remaining officers and, having explained the situation, set before them two possible alternatives - to concentrate all their efforts on walking, revitalizing and remotivating the officers and men or to go down to the whaling grounds by themselves and catch the biggest whale possible in the hope and expectation that the commotion caused would revitalise the crew.

Which plan did they adopt?

In order to try to get the best of both worlds I would encourage any church who approached me to lead a mission to consider the implications of building up the congregation in preparation for it as I intended that it should be carried out in great measure by the local church members themselves, with help from me and a few others brought in from outside. On my first visit to the leadership I began to spell out my demand for at least a year of prayer before any mission was contemplated. In the early days it was often this condition that caused kirk sessions to make polite noises but indicate 'Don't call us: we'll call you!' One of the indications of change over the years has been the difference response to this condition of prayer.

My suggested proposals were very simple: that the mission should be rooted in prayer; that the mission should be the work of the local church; that the mission was to communicate Christ and His Gospel and not the church and its organisation.

To achieve this I suggested seven phases:

PREPARATION - The informing of all the congregation of exactly what was proposed and the expectations.

TEACHING - The principles of long-term congregational mission taught from the Scriptures using existing and new forms of teaching within the congregation.

TRAINING - A specific course operated by myself over four to five weeks to give volunteers help in being able 'to give a reason for the faith that is in them'.

VISITING - Two by two, after training, often with help of people from the outside; in this area, the members of the Work and Witness organisation proved invaluable.

OUTREACH - Taking the Gospel message into every situation where the population of the area was to be found - sports grounds, bingo halls, pubs, schools, senior citizens' lunches and so on.

MAIN MEETINGS - Normally held on church premises, but with a secular flavour in order to act as a bridge between the outreach situation and a normal worship service.

FOLLOW-UP - Personal and small group care, with the stress on the probable need for new structures to accommodate new Christians.

The two phases which normally caused consternation were those of training and outreach. For many the idea of sharing their faith in words was a frightening prospect, and the concept of being trained to do that conjured up mental pictures of Jehovah's Witnesses or Moonies. It took a great deal of persuasion to bring people to the first session of the course and we have always had to stress that there was no commitment at that stage to going out on mission. I remember that the first time I used the course was at a well-known church just outside Glasgow. Some seventy people registered. One of those who came was a leader in the local Crusader class and a good friend of mine. I asked him to give me a full and frank criticism at the end of the session which deals with the qualifications of those called to be ambassadors for Christ and the motives which would be strong enough to overcome natural reticence. He looked me in the eye before I left for home that evening and said, 'Stephen, it was excellent, but far too direct. These dear folk will never be able to take that - I'll be surprised if there are more than twenty next week'. You can imagine my feelings as I drove home and prayed about the session for the following week. I entered the hall that night, in fear and trepidation, to find over one hundred people gathered. God honours His Word, and over the years I have found that the simple and direct teaching of Biblical truth, without missing out on any aspect, has its own spiritual attraction.

If the course merely attracted people it would have little value, but time and again it has been used to bring people to a new birth, into a living hope in Jesus Christ, and to experience the changed lives that accompany such faith.

It was in Barrhead that some of the most dramatic results were seen. I was thrilled on the third session there to hear a woman saying that already the subject of conversation in the supermarket was no longer the price of groceries but the Good News about Jesus. Even more thrilling was the testimony of two Church of Scotland elders who had clearly come to faith through the Scriptures, read as part of the course. At the same time a third elder in the same Church was furiously angry and accused me of proclaiming a false gospel. Part of the course consisted of homework from the Bible, and he had meticulously worked out percentages on his home computer to prove that there were more references to the Old Testament or the Epistles than to the Gospels. He was convinced that the Gospel was in the life of Jesus as portrayed in the words of the Gospel writers which we have as an example for today. My stress on the need for salvation from sin by Christ's atoning death was anathema to him. He even interrupted a meeting in one of the town churches at a later stage of the mission to object vociferously to an invitation to respond to a crucified and risen Christ. Paul wrote to the church at Corinth - 'We preach Christ and Him crucified' and this Gospel was 'the aroma of Christ among those who are being saved and those who are perishing. To the one we are the smell of death, to the other the fragrance of life'. The Gospel is like Marmite - you either hate it or love it.

In the early days I was concerned about the length of time which it would take for those on the course to do their homework. At the second session at a church in Prestwick I asked people to say how long it had taken them. One man brought up in the Brethren said he had done it in twenty minutes, at which I noticed a young couple looking at each other and smiling shyly and broadly. I asked them how long they had taken and they said, 'We are new Christians as well as being newly married. We started to do the course together in bed at 11 o'clock one night - and put the light out at 3.30 the next morning!' I was horrified, and said so, but they both protested strongly 'Oh, no - we loved it; we just got carried away by the Bible and couldn't put it down!' Oh, that many of us might find that thrill in the Word of God!

The initial response to the training was nothing compared with the response to any suggestion that people should actually go into pubs or bingo halls to share their faith. Having been in the army, I can only described the attitude as one of mutiny. Nevertheless, many overcame their fears and shyness and to their amazement found that not only were customers far less hostile or apathetic than expected but that they were given words to say and new Christlike attitudes as they spoke, so that they came home like the early disciples, rejoicing. It was a straight-laced minister who agreed to enter a pub for the first time in his life, and spoke of a freedom and a joy that he had never known before when he eventually returned to the church at closing-time.

Perhaps it is significant that these two phases, both of which are concerned with a person to person sharing of the faith, raised most concern. Satan knows the most effective methods of making inroads into his territory and will not let them go ahead without interference.

Chapter 8

SCOTROC-THE SOUND OF MUSIC AND THE PULL OF DRAMA

I had been called by God to be an evangelist at a University Mission, so youth clearly played an important role in my thinking. In the late sixties, during the early days of my ministry, youth was in ferment: revolutionary attitudes were shown not only in the rejection of authority but above all in that rejection of the acceptance of injustice and resistance to change which was irrevocably associated in the minds and spirits of young folk with 'the establishment'. That establishment clearly included the Church. The philosophy of the time was expressed in the lyrics of the songs, with their underlying pessimism and cynicism. 'The answer, my friend, is blowing in the wind' echoed the disillusioned cry of the writer of Ecclesiastes: 'Everything is meaningless, a chasing after the wind'.

Increasingly philosophies were being communicated through the words of the songs. The prophets to youth for almost thirty years have been the lyric writers and the disc jockeys, and their overriding message of despair and cynicism has gone almost unchallenged.

Early on I saw the need to enlist the media of music and drama in the cause of Christ. Almost immediately this caused problems, because artists are sensitive people: the idea of their arts' being 'prostituted' for the sake of anything other than that art itself caused hurt pride and a feeling of lost integrity. In the field of music evangelicals had often used musicians in their 'softening up' process to induce an emotional atmosphere where the spoken word could not only be received but could induce a response at least partly motivated by that emotional atmosphere. The younger generation of Christian musicians recognizing the danger of this becoming one of the worldly underhand methods renounced by the apostle Paul, and being extremely jealous of their own musical integrity, found it very difficult to work in an evangelistic situation and thus often opted for a purely musical performance, trusting that their own witness as Christians in the music world would count for Christ. In some cases - and the most notable example is Cliff Richard - this has been honoured of God, but sadly in many cases the spiritual has been lost as the emphasis has been transferred to the musical. The Christian music scene in Scotland is littered with the spiritual graves of disillusioned young musicians.

In the same way Christian drama, which became acceptable again after many years only in the 1970's, fell into a similar dilemma. Was it valid to go into the secular world of drama as a Christian? Did Christian drama always have to include at least some aspect of Christian truth? Could drama by itself be used for communicating the Gospel? These and other questions are still very much to the fore and continue to arouse strong feelings; but this is not the place to elaborate upon these issues. In my own ministry I was convinced that both music and drama were legitimate means of communicating the Gospel but they could never replace the preaching of the Word - 'the simple proclamation of the truth'. I read, however, of Ezekiel's dramatisation of the siege of Jerusalem, and of Jeremiah's dramatic use of his loin-cloth as a visual aid, and was convinced that God did not spurn the use of the dramatic. This conviction was encouraged by two events at an Easter mission in Stewarton.

The first was in the church on a Sunday morning before the mission when I preached from Jeremiah 13 and had a pair of underpants ready as a visual aid. The first pair held up were brand-new but, as Jeremiah had actually done, I pretended to bury them and then dig them up again later to find that they were good for nothing. The pair that I extracted from the bottom of the pulpit had been buried in a mixture of acid, old oil and peat, and the effect when they were thrown down into the church was electric and lasting. The point was grasped that we who were created to be as intimate with God as one's personal clothing were now spoiled by sin and good for nothing. The second incident took place in the working men's club that Easter Sunday afternoon. There was a 'talent show' amongst the three hundred people who were present, and we had obtained permission for Albert Bogle, who is now a minister of the Church of Scotland but was then a student and a member of the mission team, to sing two Easter songs. As he started I saw the electric organist lean back cynically and light a cigarette. Then something happened, and the organist put down his cigarette and quietly started to play. Albert allowed the guitar to hang loosely from its strap around his neck, and a pin could have been heard drop as three hundred people listened, in hushed attendance, to the words sung to a modern tune: 'There was none other good enough to pay the price of sin, He only could unlock the gate of heaven and let us in'.

As the value of both music and drama, especially in the field of youth evangelism, became more apparent, there arose a major problem regarding performers being available at suitable times. A mission to Bannockburn concentrated on youth and had much of its emphasis in the High School, with the willing support of the headmaster and Religious Education staff. It was here that the problem of availability was brought to a head.

The interest had mounted as the week proceeded and it was clear that some lunch-time event on the Friday would draw large numbers. To find suitable artists at such short notice for a performance in the middle of the day called for much prior planning - and considerable telephoning. The concert filled the hall to overflowing, and after a short explanation of the Gospel I invited those really interested to leave the hall and meet me outside while the concert continued through two final songs. One be one fifty-four pupils came to enquire about becoming Christians and that day and over the weekend were counselled and led to Christ. There was, alas, considerable opposition, and the minister's life was made almost unbearable. The group have now been scattered to the four winds, but nevertheless it was clear that effective evangelism had taken place and the Sovereign God had used music and drama, together with the preaching of His Word, to bring people to a living faith.

Scotroc - The sound of music and the pull of drama

Soon after that I was involved in British Youth for Christ in Scotland and came in touch with one of their musical evangelists, who was an extremely talented guitarist and songwriter and who was looking for an opening in Scotland. We joined forces and recruited a small team of volunteers for one year. Stuck for a name we adopted that of Scotroc, this being due partly to the nature of the music and partly to Christ being the only rock on which Scotland can truly stand.

The whole concept of the team was that members would be gifted in music or drama up to a professional standard and would volunteer for one year's service with expenses only being paid, and board and lodging provided only when on mission. The early days were traumatic. Personalities clashed louder than cymbals; leadership was questioned or resented; the car and trailer, purchased from an account aided by the Church of Scotland Home Board and a Christian trust, were scarcely fit for the demands put upon them; team members arrived late and depressingly cold after a long journey and various breakdowns, often to be met by an angry and anxious leader. It was a miracle that God was able to use us at all.

Tensions between musicians are often bad enough, but when drama is included the area for disagreement is even greater. Most of the music had been written by two of the members of the team in strongly contrasting styles; the sketches - most of which I had written myself - not only varied in quality but were received with varying degrees of enthusiasm by team members. I now know what an author feels like when a piece of work, which he considers excellent, is scathingly rejected and discarded in favour of another piece which he feels is quite tasteless. I am sure that my feelings were echoed by others on the team. Yet God held us together and used us over the years; teams changed, but the basic pattern remained fairly constant.

Perhaps the introduction of a new member to the team was one of the most traumatic times, and I think of four such incidents. For example a gifted young bass guitar player was due to join the first Scotroc team and he accompanied us to Strathpeffer, where a youth concert was planned for the pavilion in April. It was freezing cold and there was no heating in the hall. The drummer built his kit on blocks centre stage which ensured that the full volume blasted into the ear of the bass player. The invitation to respond to the Gospel provoked an immediate response, so that the majority of the audience left for the counselling room during the last song, at a point when the stage lights had to be taken down in order to provide lighting for the counselling room. No food was provided, and tempers flared as we tried to clear up, with some of the audience seeking spiritual counsel and others wanting to hear more of the band or get on to the drum kit. The miracle was that the bass player survived for a full year.

He came in at the deep end, and survived: others simply could not start. In the early days I advertised for team members in various Christian magazines and had plenty of replies. Most were clearly unsuitable but one young man seemed well qualified, so I asked him to join us for a weekend mission in Govan. He was an excellent musician but, it seemed, had expected to play before a douce crowd of well-behaved churchgoing people. A lunch-time concert in Govan High School and an evening in the church hall with the local gang was more than he had expected, and he left us a sadder, but perhaps wiser, young man, with a new, very different view of evangelism.

Jane was due to make up a small team, and joined us for a trial week at a youth mission in Falkirk. On the second day she was carrying across the school playground some four hundred slides, carefully packed in magazines for tape slide presentation. Her face as she tripped and scattered the slides over yards of playground still comes to my memory. She had obviously heard of my former temper, and expected an outburst thereof, which I freely admit was only restrained by the powerful grace of God.

Alison was a drama student who accompanied her friend Jane to an interview. Jane had heard of the vacancy through her father, who had been at a presbytery meeting and thought the job sounded suitable for her. It soon became clear that Jane, although a church-goer, was not a Christian, but that Alison had been praying for her for months. As the interview proceeded in the Youth Theatre in Glasgow the subject was not drama but Christ, and before we parted Jane had given her life to Jesus and received him as Saviour and Lord. Her fresh, inquisitive mind and spirit were to be greatly valued in our team Bible studies together over that year. With two professional dramatists, a man with experience in the same field and just one girl musician, the emphasis that year was clearly on drama, and it included the making of a video in conjunction with the Scripture Union.

Drama is a strange and powerful medium but it is easily misunderstood. Many of the sketches were based on the parables of Jesus, sometimes with a different and dramatic ending. Such was 'The Prodigal Daughter' where the repentant, returning daughter is seen from a long distance by her mother. They come together, running in slow motion, to the tune of 'Chariots of Fire' and the mother slaps her daughter to the ground and turns on her heel with the words, 'You deserved that!' In some church circles this left the audience totally bewildered, but it certainly drew attention in places like pubs. This sort of bewilderment was perhaps best expressed by an ex-moderator of the Church of Scotland. I had written an article in 'Life and Work' purporting to be classified files from the 'new church selection board' showing that whilst Lydia and Paul (names having been disguised) had been accepted, Peter and Jesus were turned down. The eminent churchman complained about the inappropriateness of confidential Church documents being leaked and quoted.

In recent years the arts have been increasingly recognized as having a part to play in God's economy, and it is interesting to note that this is not new but a return to the views expressed by Calvin at the time of the Reformation, although practice of the arts was limited by the licentious attitudes associated with the theatre of that culture. I believe that this use of drama in proclamation and evangelism is entirely Biblical, and that most of the objections raised by those in the Church are cultural rather than scriptural. It is, of course, possible to go too far and to give offence - and this has clearly happened in some areas in the realm of worship - but let us beware of throwing the baby out with the bathwater and turning our backs on a legitimate method of helping those outside the Kingdom to respond to Christ and His Gospel. Scotroc made many mistakes and may at times have given unnecessary offence, for which we are truly sorry, but there has been much of God in the formation and use of this team and I sincerely hope that the underlying principles will continue in the service of Christ and His Church.

Having the Scotroc team inevitably changed the pattern of the ministry to some extent, but many of the thrills and spills of mission remained exactly the same. One of the problems which often arose when a combined mission was proposed was whom to include and whom to exclude. I usually found that if I met the leaders early on, during the planning stage, and made clear that I would be proclaiming a Biblical Gospel of salvation, leading to a new life, then that Gospel itself constituted a dividing line. Yet even after that there could be problems.

In Dumfries in 1981 this had been the procedure carried out, and as a result a number of individual Roman Catholics joined the mission wholeheartedly although the two churches of their denomination stood apart. Two incidents reveal the dilemma which still faces those who would want all Christians to work together for the cause of Gospel but are not prepared to sacrifice truth.

The prayer convener was a Roman Catholic layman. Neither the local Brethren nor the Free Church took exception to this deeply spiritual man, but a local extreme Protestant group was appalled, and picketed the church and hall where the meetings were being held. I pleaded with them not to judge before hearing the evidence, and warmly invited them to attend a meeting and then meet with us to discuss the content of the message proclaimed. The invitation was rejected with some invective, and the only factor that they seemed to consider relevant was that one of the organisers was a member of the Roman Catholic Church. I found this association difficult to reconcile with a Biblical Gospel, but the man concerned is responsible for his actions to God and not to any of us.

It is interesting to note that Luther and Calvin recognized that there were Christians in the Roman Catholic Church in their day: it seems that some of their followers are less discerning. The picketing became increasingly intense, but quite inadvertently I discovered the answer. To accommodate everyone, the last evening meeting was to be held in a different location, and as I approached I was handed a tract outside the door. Naively thinking that this was a Christian taking the opportunity to share Gospel literature I thanked the man, shook his hand, called him my brother and asked God to bless him. The man was so taken aback that my party and a good number of others behind entered the hall without the usual shouts of abuse. Without my realising it God had used the principle of His word, 'A soft answer turns away wrath'. I am not saying that relationships with the Roman Catholics were of that woolly ecumenical variety that tolerates everything; but the truth in this situation was clear that to turn our backs upon that individual would have been to grieve the Holy Spirit. The counselling convener of that same mission was an elder in the Brethren, a local headmaster and a godly man with a very clear understanding of sound doctrine. Three monks and two nuns working at St Joseph's School applied to be counsellors for us. The convener was really 'put on the spot', prayed much and consulted with myself and others. Eventually we decided that the crucial issue would be the doctrine of justification by faith alone, and so I was commissioned to spend the whole of one of the training sessions on that subject.

That night I expounded the doctrine from Paul's letter to the Galatians and went to immense lengths to make it absolutely clear that the ground we stood on was based on the Reformed tradition and the Westminster Confession of Faith. After one and a half hours and some detailed questions, the senior priest shook me warmly by the hand and said, 'That is exactly what we ought to believe!' Surely Luther and Calvin rejoiced in heaven.

It has not always been like that. I recall sending a note to a priest in Carfin that some of his flock had professed conversion and would be receiving follow-up material. He wrote asking to see the leaflets, and later asked for fifty copies to be sent that he might use with his youth fellowship. But six weeks or so later he was moved out of Scotland and has never been heard of since.

There is still an intransigence about much of the hierarchy, and much of the teaching is destructive, if not damnable. A woman was visited in her home by a member of the Work and Witness team who were involved in the mission to Cambusbarron, just outside Stirling. She was extremely interested, and attended each one of the meetings held in the hall. After the last meeting she came to me with tears in her eyes and said, 'How I wish I could believe what you have being saying. I long to be able to speak with God, but all my life I have been brought up to believe that I have to pray to a saint who may eventually hear me and who then has to carry my request to God or to Mary, which may take months or even years'. I showed her the Word of God, saying that through Christ we both have access to the Father by one Spirit: but the accumulated indoctrination of years had done its dire work and she went away very sorrowful. What a heavy responsibility lies on those who taught her that dreadful doctrine.

Because of these attitudes to the truth my policy has been to welcome Roman Catholics who love the Lord Jesus and His Biblical Gospel, but not to stand on the same platform as a representative of a Church which denies the ultimate authority of the revelation of Scripture. This position has provoked attack from both directions, which I have accepted as having at any rate some sort of Biblical balance.

There were times when a mission was used to bring a measure, at least, of reconciliation between warring factions. Caldercruix in Lanarkshire is renowned for the bitterness between the Orange and Green communities. The outreach phase of the mission included visits to all pubs in the village. We were scheduled to visit two on Thursday evening, and were warned that they were at opposite ends of the social scale.

The first was a veritable 'howff', with space for about eighteen customers taken up by the total clientele that night, which numbered three. The roof was leaking and the smell indescribable. The team was not too disappointed when we had to move on, especially as one member had stood with a drip leaking on his head throughout the presentation. The second establishment was completely packed out, but as we entered I noticed a nine-foot gap in the middle of the bar. When I queried this I was given a strange look and told briefly that the Catholics were on the right and the Orangemen on the left.... and between them was a great gulf like that separating heaven from hell.

We had decided to start with a raucous, zany and somewhat outrageous sketch involving two monkeys, and to my horror I saw the two girls with their monkey masks leaping on to pool tables. I expected a fearsome row, but instead there was a marked attention: as the two sketches led into three songs and a word from the Scriptures a hush fell over the whole crowded room; suddenly I noticed that the gap no longer existed! As the presentation finished, and Gospels were offered by the team and local Christians, so conversation started and some thirty minutes later I saw that the whole crowd was now in groups, Roman Catholics mixing with Protestants and all asking questions and sharing spiritual truth with the team members. My group was turned out at closing-time and we continued talking in the car park long into the night, eventually drifting home with many of the Catholics carrying a John's Gospel (in an orange cover) and many an Orangemen carrying a Mark's Gospel (in a green cover). And the God of gentle humour smiled.

Once Scotroc became established, it was easier to devise some pattern for the ten to fourteen day period of outreach and mission which made up two of the phases in a congregational mission. Whatever the programmes for the day, we ensured a time for the team to meet for Bible study and prayer. Often we were joined by local Christians, which gave a wonderful opportunity to deepen fellowship. These times were very precious, and I became increasingly aware that much of the spiritual work of evangelism was forged during them.

We sought to make contact with all of school age during the day, as well as to visit such places as educational centres, factories and DSS centres at lunch-time. In primary schools we would normally be granted a half-hour with each age group, and would vary the programme according to the age of the children. In each case, however, it would include some drama by the team, often involving a considerable amount of humour, some chorus singing and generally an 'epic'. This was an Old Testament story dramatised and using the children, directed by the team members. David and Goliath were favourites, and the war cries of the Israelites and the Philistines could be heard many classrooms away. But the real favourite was probably the story of 'King Nebby' and the three (or was it four?) men in the Fiery Furnace. Getting the children to participate always went down well with both pupils and teachers.

Secondary schools presented a different challenge. We sought to visit Religious Education or social education classes, or to hold at least two lunch-time concerts in the school hall or some similar areas near the dining-hall. In early days the spectre of proselytism reared its ugly head, and we had to ensure a programme that was acceptable to school staff. In the classroom this normally took the form of the team's acting out one of Jesus' parables in modern guise, (for instance the story of the elder daughter's smashing her father's brand new Mercedes, and, and having been forgiven, then furiously attacking her younger sister who had broken a wheel on her borrowed bicycle), after which we would read another parable and invite the class to break into groups in order to write and perform a sketch along similar lines.

The non-doctrinaire approach, with pupil participation, calmed the fears of many teachers, although there were always some who were bitterly opposed to any Gospel input. This opposition was beautifully countered by the Lord, who caused the secretary of the Head Teachers' Association to see us at work in his school. He was extremely pleased with the effect of the team - I think he saw it chiefly in terms of educational communication - and being a real enthusiast invited me to speak at the conference of Head Teachers at St Andrews that year and to show a

111

video made by Scotroc. This broke the ice amongst many head teachers, and I found a ready welcome and a good response from then on.

Although direct evangelism was clearly impossible in the classroom, yet pupils were exposed to the Gospel and attracted by the team and the presentation. As a result many would flock to the lunch-time concert. I think especially of the school at East Kilbride where we were not expected to fill more than half the theatre, but had to have entry by ticket only for the second and third day because numbers had to be restricted for safety reasons. At these concerts a clear presentation of the Gospel was given and pupils invited to respond by coming forward at the end to receive a copy of John's Gospel with the booklet 'Journey into Life' printed at the back. In order to prevent pupils from taking the book and then throwing it away they had to give a note of their name and class, and this list was handed to the chaplain and the leader of the local Scripture Union Group.

We saw this system as rather like a potato riddle. Those who came to the lunch-time concert showed some response; those who took a booklet went a step further, and the next step for many was either to attend the Scripture Union group or to attend the concert in the church hall at the end of the week, when a clear invitation to receive Christ would be given.

When Scotroc and I were invited to Shetland for the first Church of Scotland presbytery mission we were somewhat apprehensive, but in the end the only man who had his fears realised was the team member who disliked sea travel - and found a lot of ferries in

Shetland!

The response on the islands was tremendously encouraging and we saw God clearly at work amongst both young and old. Perhaps the most significant feature of the whole mission was to see Shetlanders going to share their faith in Christ with their neighbours in the same parish. Three incidents stand out. Firstly, the warmth of the welcome by the islanders was matched by the warmth of the tribute paid to the team at the General Assembly that year; secondly, there was the strange anomaly of the minister who spoke and wrote enthusiastically of the mission but took me aside just before the final rally to ask me to leave out 'that born again stuff'; and thirdly, the incident which provided the title of this book. We had returned to a manse on the mainland after a hectic day, involving four ferry crossings and five Gospel presentations, including preaching. As I longed for bed at 11.45 that evening, the minister, a master chef, started to create an exotic French sauce, to go with the large quantity of mussels he had obtained on his way through Lerwick. 'Mussels at Midnight' still sends shivers down my spine and strange sensations into my stomach.

Towards the end of the Scotroc ministry, two missions stand out within the overall plan of God. One was at Fortrose and Rosemarkie, where three denominations came together and the Gospel was communicated to all ages. An overwhelming response in the local Academy saw many come to the Lord, and one of the most apparently unlikely pupils is now a bright light shining for God. For a considerable time after the mission, staff and pupils were gathering together to pray at lunch-time. Amongst adults too the Spirit was at work, and Moray Firth Radio carried an hour-long programme testifying to the effects of the mission and perhaps the surprise of many that the churches could be seen and heard working together - and even taking the Gospel into the local pubs.

On the last evening of that mission a 'Christian ceilidh' was scheduled for the evening in Rosemarkie hall. Hostesses were asked to invite their friends and bring a basket supper. Tea and coffee were provided, and some sixty seats had been set out around tables. As the starting time approached many tables had to be removed and replaced by chairs as more and more people arrived - until we even ran out of cups! After that evening a man who had lived in the area all his life said in amazement that he had never seen such a cross-section of the whole community under one roof before. Surely the Gospel is the agent of God's call to reconciliation and true community.

The old parish church in Larbert was to be scene of the last Scotroc mission, although the team came together finally for a highly successful and much appreciated repeat visit to the girls of Kilgraston Convent School. The prayer and planning had been meticulous, and six people had professed conversion during phases leading up to the outreach and main meetings. The faithful prayer and work of the congregation were rewarded by God, and the Lord added daily to that church those who were being saved.

There stands out in my memory one incident

during a visit to one of the pubs, at the Cross. A man came in and listened very intently. When approached and asked why he had come that evening his reply was, 'I heard you were coming so I came to find God'. How thrilling that God had drawn him to reach after truth, but how sad that he felt he had to come to the pub rather than to the church to do so!

Chapter 9

DOUBTS - FIGHTINGS AND FEARS

In 1977 I was much involved in the building of the new Christian ski centre which I described in the chapter about ski-ing. This was Kincraig in Badenoch and Strathspey.

As the building progressed it became increasingly urgent to decide who was to be the warden in charge. Because of the situation in the parish it was felt that the minister of Alvie and Insh should take on the task, with much of the work being done by someone experienced in the outdoor activity scene. And so it was decided that I should be appointed as evangelist to Speyside, with special reference to skiers in the Badenoch Christian Centre; indeed, at one meeting the minister agreed that he would not insist on being the warden and I was appointed to the post, but two days later, before the minutes were published, the decision was rescinded; the local minister felt that this parish would inevitably be linked with a neighbouring one if the two jobs were not combined.

Meanwhile the family were delighted at the thought of a move to the Aviemore area but I had a feeling that it was too good to be true, and that somehow God could not have it in His will for us to go to a place which would cater for so many of our human desires. Worried about this, and the whole question of guidance, I went to see my minister in Edinburgh. Jim Philip had always recommended that major decisions should be shared with the fellowship in prayer, and so I described the circumstances to him, and asked him to take the matter to the prayer meeting. To my consternation his reply was almost brusque. 'I will not', he said. 'Stephen, what sort of a God do you worship?'

He had so clearly seen that my hesitation was entirely due to a false image of our Heavenly Father - seeing Him as One who delights in frustrating us rather than One who delights in giving good gifts to His children. Of course there are times when we reach the Kingdom 'through many hardships', but our God is no sadistic tyrant.

All the pieces of the jigsaw fitted neatly into place. We sold our Edinburgh house in a very short space of time and were the only people to offer for Alltnacriche - a beautiful house set in seventeen acres of land some one-and-a-half miles into deep country, behind Aviemore. It had been designed and built by Sir George Henschel, a well-known musician. He had designed a magnificent house, built in the Austrian style, in a superb setting, with a large music-room some thirty yards away from the house. Perhaps his wife had forbidden him to compose within earshot!

We saw this as ideal for Christian gatherings. The whole place exuded peace, and at first sight we felt that this was the place God wanted to use to spread His peace. The nature of the house and grounds and its location seemed just right to use as a place where troubled folk could come, share in our family life and find in the physical quiet the spiritual peace that comes only from being justified by faith through our

Lord Jesus Christ.

I was duly appointed to the Presbytery of Abernethy, and we moved in September. Later that month I was involved with a youth fellowship - at their own request - when they were staying at the Badenoch Christian Centre. I showed two film strips which I had made myself, including one on the subject of judgement. The minister, who had not been informed or consulted, was furious, and firmly forbade me ever to enter the centre again. I felt as if I had been hit in the solar plexus by the heavyweight champion of the world, and lay awake for nights with a deep sinking feeling inside. All sorts of feelings of self-justification, anger, hurt, disappointment and questioning festered within me, and though I found in the Psalms much to which I could relate, yet at the time this was of little comfort.

A few weeks later I attended my first presbytery meeting and was firmly told that I would, under no circumstances, work in any parish in the presbytery until I had been invited by the minister and kirk session. Ministers were invited to get in touch with me forthwith, and I waited expectantly. Weeks passed, and not a single invitation was received. Just as when I had been banned from the centre, doubts came thrusting in and depression hung heavy about me; although outwardly I probably showed little, inwardly there was a great difficulty in the exercise of faith.

Eventually I was asked to attend a meeting of the session of Rothiemurchus and Aviemore. In the course of my setting out what I believed God was calling me to do I gave my own testimony, which included the fact that I had been an elder before being a Christian. After a very short discussion I was told that I could work on Cairngorm but not come near any other part of the parish without express permission.

Two days later I was called in by the minister, who spoke angrily of my having disturbed his elders. He told me that one of them had come to him deeply convicted and disturbed in spirit but that he had been able to dismiss that man's fears. This was said in such a way that it was quite clear that they had been airily dismissed as being unreal. My heart was almost broken, and I went home with deep anger and sorrow, and a desperate sense of hurt and rejection. I was quite sure that the Spirit had been convincing that man of his need of Jesus. I realised that God was pointing out once again, as He had pointed out in the Old Testament, that the priests were 'healing the wounds of My people lightly'. But the other half of me brought self-accusation - that it was my offence, and not the offence of the Gospel. Doubts about my methods of communicating the Gospel split over into doubts about the content of the Gospel itself. Was I standing firm for the truth, or merely standing out against the tide? Was my gospel the true Good News of love as strong as death, or was it harsh and denying the true love of Christ?

And so began months of real agony of spirit. Convinced that we had been called of God - as well as being called by the presbytery - we now found every door slammed in our faces. A very small group of understanding Christians met monthly to pray with us but otherwise the rejection was complete.

The hurt was two-fold. Firstly in the area of rejection: I now realise that some of this was due to pride, and that God's painful breaking purposes had to involve circumstances such as these; but the human pain, and the longing to withdraw into a shell of indifference, was almost overwhelming.

The second and perhaps the more serious attack was in the realm of faith itself, both about the nature of the Gospel and in the area of guidance. Why had God called and then apparently abandoned? Had He really called at all? Were we guided by human circumstances and therefore out of the will of God? These and similar questions had bombarded my mind and spirit until I was almost reduced to despair. On many an occasion it was only my wife's faith that kept us going. Joy insisted that we had been called of God and were simply being asked to exercise our faith under a situation of trial so that we might learn to rejoice in the certainty that everything works together for the good of those who love God and are called according to His purpose. That lesson had to be learned the hard way; for me, at least, the learning was delayed by my own slowness to learn, appreciate and accept. I would see the faults in those round about and in the system which had brought about this traumatic situation; but looking at others, and at the negative features, I failed to look at God - and especially to the Cross of Jesus, from which perspective alone can there be any understanding about such situations and any acceptance of God within them.

The battle was not easy, and certainly not short. Days and weeks turned into months of doubt and depression, but gradually God's Spirit prevailed. I noticed that the whole atmosphere in Speyside was beginning to change as more and more Christians came to the valley and met to worship and to pray. The summer mission team stayed in our home for six weeks at a time and brought joy and spiritual vitality, not only into our home but into the various places where mission activities took place throughout the valley. Leading that team and ministering to them through the morning Bible studies was a tremendous encouragement, as God clearly showed that He was still at work, and using my ministry, so that I began to recognise that He had not abandoned us. The other aspect of encouraging work at this time was the parking of 'His Van' in the Corrie Cas Car Park, which provided a focal point for Christian witness for skiers, and where some real spiritual work in the caravan showed that God had not abandoned His cause or His servant. The light began to appear at the end of the tunnel.

It was at this time that Alltnacriche was used to help those who came to stay - and generally there was a mutual encouragement. Very early a young man appeared, having worked in a kibbutz in Israel. He had been on mission with me in the past, and his farming background was of great value: he replaced all the fences to keep in the fifteen or twenty ewes that we kept for a number of reasons - to retain an interest in farming, to keep the grass down and to provide the sort of situation where those emotionally disturbed could find that in looking after animals they could experience a new dimension, which would overflow into the spiritual. The young man's enthusiastic faith was a great help to us, and I trust that he looks upon his present calling as a parish minister with equal joy.

Some visitors were of a difference nature. I think of the second-year student who arrived at the end of her tether, with threats of suicide. The strain of an English course studying Sarte, Camus and other existentialist philosophers and trying to reconcile their thinking with Biblical truth was too much for her brain. I learned a great deal from trying to deal with this particular student. I found that it was not the counselling sessions in my study which really helped her but simply living in the country and sharing with Joy over the kitchen sink. She later testified that it was the sheer routine of a Christian family home that was used in her healing. Biblical truth certainly needs to be made in words to affect our thinking so that we take every thought captive to Christ; but Biblical truth needs to be lived and experienced if it is really to heal our spirits.

I think also of a Jamaican woman who was sent to us from Edinburgh. She gave the impression of being a deeply moral, Christian woman, but inside there was frightful evil, and I believe now that she was possessed by evil spirits. Under the guise of being helpful, she continually tried to undermine the relationship between Joy and myself. On one occasion she told me, with obvious enjoyment, (although outward shock), that Joy had revealed some of her underclothing in the presence of Robin Mabbolt, an ex-drug addict who was staying at our house. The whole way in which she related the story was clearly designed to make me feel jealous and angry against my wife. We discussed the matter that evening, and had a good laugh as we found that in fact she had been showing something to her mother, who was in the room at the time when Robin had happened to come in. Laughter dispelled that attack but there was a continuing and constant sense of evil as long as she remained in the home; eventually we had to allow her to depart as Lucy, our youngest daughter, could no longer sleep for fear when the woman was in the house. With greater experience I would now confront those evil forces in the name of Jesus, in a more forcible and direct manner, but at the time, although we saw only partial victory, it was a further sign of God's not having withdrawn His presence.

Increasingly it became clear that although God had a work for me in Spey Valley, yet He also wanted me to resume a travelling ministry. Considerable numbers of invitations confirmed that call and so a pattern emerged: missions throughout Scotland in the spring and autumn, with preparatory classes run at other times of the year; the summer mission to Speyside in July and August; and the ski ministry from January to April, which developed into my working as a full-time instructor with the Abernethy Christian Outdoor Centre.

And so the phase of our life in Aviemore, which had started with such high hopes and had seen the dashing of those hopes and a period of depression and trauma, developed into a combination of home-based and travelling evangelism which was surely a preparation for the phase to follow. Sometimes the impression given is that the Christian life is well guarded from the problems that come to all human beings, or at least that the Christian is immune from the inner problems whilst facing the outward ones. This has not been the experience of many who were used to write the very Scriptures of God. It has not been the experience of godly men and women down through the centuries, nor has it been my experience; but I can say with the same grasp of truth and assurance of faith that was expressed by the apostle Paul that I can now see how such trials can be used of God to strengthen both character and hope.

There is of course considerable danger in dwelling on the difficulties and inner tensions of the Christian life, but I believe that Jesus never hesitated to invite men to consider the cost of commitment to Him; and I am convinced that that cost is more likely to involve the struggles of the soul than the sacrifice of material things. Christians have been guilty of saying little about such times for fear of putting off unbelievers or young Christians. We have felt that to admit to such feelings and experiences would somehow deny the peace that is the promise of the Gospel. But our God is the God who is truth, and He cannot honour deception in any form.

My experience at this time confirms the truth of Scripture that we are involved in a spiritual battle and that the victory is by no means immediate. But I would also testify to the extraordinary paradox that at the same time as this testing and trauma of faith, there was, and still exists at a far deeper level, a peace that is neither dependent upon feelings nor governed by circumstances, which is beyond not only our understanding but also our verbal expression. That is the promised peace of Jesus, and it can and does undergird the struggles of the soul and the spiritual battles which we are bound to experience in this world where the authority of the Prince of Peace is not yet fully recognized or acknowledged.

Chapter 10

ALL OVER THE WORLD GOD'S SPIRIT IS MOVING

I had travelled so much in my army days that I felt I never wanted to go abroad again after we settled into farming. But it was not to be. Perhaps the settled life, despite its many advantages, can lead in to a rut of normality so that we forget that as Christians we are always on the move spiritually and that as pilgrims and strangers in this world we are not to settle down in what is no continuing city. Whatever the cause, God soon had me moving around the country as a travelling evangelist, and gave me the further great privilege of going across the sea to other lands on a number of occasions.

My first invitation to Northern Ireland came from a young people's convention in Londonderry. T.S. Mooney, a banker and Crusader leader, was the secretary, and also my host. A truly remarkable man, with a breadth of vision, and a warmth of Christian love which so graciously commended his firm evangelical convictions, he also had a sense of humour that could be highly disconcerting. He was a very fast and somewhat erratic driver so that I spent a good deal of our first journey from Aldergrove airport to Londonderry in fervent prayer. Approaching one sharp corner, at tremendous speed, I was highly relieved to see a narrow track providing an escape route of which we duly took advantage. That night I used the incident as an example of how God always provides a way of escape from sin. There was an appreciative roar of laughter from the hundreds of young people at the convention, but I was not quite sure how T.S. would take it or whether I would be welcomed in his home. I was, indeed, privileged to be his friend over many years, but he never learned to slow down when behind the wheel of a car. He constantly reminded me of that incident when we first met, and would deny emphatically that he had been driving too fast!

From the first visit, two incidents stand out with regard to the troubles there. On the first evening we had gathered for prayer in a house on the outskirts of Londonderry when a tremendous explosion shook the whole area. My instinctive reaction was to fling myself behind the large sofa. No one else moved or stopped praying. Somewhat sheepishly I settled down again but was scarcely reassured by the comment at the end of the prayer time - 'That would be the petrol station at the corner of the road again. That's the fourth time this year'.

The other incident also took place that evening, as we drove towards the Waterside where the convention was being held. We were stopped by the police and delayed for some fifteen minutes. As we were allowed to proceed, I saw a human hand lying in the gutter close to the shattered remains of the RUC constable's car. Many of the young people attending the convention walked past it apparently unmoved.

I suppose the hardening effect of constant violence is inevitable, but what a tragedy that the warm-hearted Irish, gifted with so much Christian understanding and zeal, should lose the sensitivity of Christ, or rather should have had to build a protective layer of hardness to prevent that sensitivity from being broken and crushed.

It was this mixture of Christlike understanding and love and rank bigotry and hardness which struck me in the face and has continued to give me great concern during repeated visits over the years. A Biblical Christianity that leaves the heart unmoved and the attitude to others unchanged must be suspect, and this dichotomy between belief and behaviour is perhaps nowhere more clearly seen than in certain areas of Ulster evangelicalism.

A minister friend of mine, who was exchanging pulpits for six months, attended the morning and evening services in a well-known church in Belfast on his Sunday off. I met him three days later still apparently suffering from shock. 'In the morning', he said, 'I heard the Gospel preached as clearly and as winsomely as ever in my life. It was like being in heaven. At night it was a tirade and I have never been more aware of the presence of evil'.

These things ought not to be.

Let me not be all negative! I have a deep love for Ulster and its people, and have many glorious memories of Christians who have both the mind and the Spirit of Christ. In an age of bigotry it is hard to show love without being accused of compromising the truth, but it can be done in the power of the Spirit, and I have been thrilled to be associated with many Biblical ministries where the truth is carefully guarded and faithfully preached, accompanied by a warmth and acceptance of others which beautifully commends the Gospel of Christ. Bigotry and hatred make the news, but the signs of the Kingdom are being shown in the lives of many Christians in Ulster who will never be accorded recognition by the media.

I believe this is especially true amongst the younger generation. I had been privileged to attend 'Youth Reach' on two occasions. This four-day gathering of young Presbyterians at the University of Ulster in Coleraine attracts many hundreds of young folk, and a mixture of exuberant praise and solid Bible teaching provides exciting fare. I think of one evening when a young minister brought together on the platform a Presbyterian prison officer and a Roman Catholic ex-convict. Both had received Christ as Saviour and Lord, and it was deeply moving not only to see and hear them express the reality of a unity in Christ but also to sense the change of attitude amongst the young audience, who had inherited prejudices and bigotries which melted in the light of God's truth and love. Surely that spirit of uncompromising truth and Holy Spirit love is the only hope for that weary province. There is that hope!

Perhaps the original invitation to Northern Ireland came because of the close links between Scots and the Irish; it was my connection with the armed forces that led to an invitation by the officers' Christian Union to tour various military bases of the British Army of the Rhine and speak to groups of officers, soldiers and their families of my faith in the Lord Jesus.

It was strange to return to many of the places where I had served in my military days. It was even more strange to see the whole military scene from a totally different perspective. Some things had not changed one iota, but others were completely different.

On my first visit I was accompanied by a senior officer stationed at the Ministry of Defence, who had allocated two weeks of his annual leave to this trip and the ensuing week to a ski-house party with cadets and young officers from Sandhurst. Brigadier Ian Dobbie is a highly professional soldier with a very proper sense of discipline and decorum, and it was strange to go back to wondering whether my shoes were highly enough polished and my suit of a suitable hue. We developed a deep friendship as he drove me across Europe and I came to recognize the extra dimension of Christian maturity that real discipline can give. Two of the areas which inevitably cause problems in the minds of young Christians who consider the army as a calling are the morality of war and the 'class distinction' between officer and other ranks. With regard to the morality of war, I can only say that whilst I wholeheartedly respect those Christians who see pacifism as the only option in the light of Christ's individual example and His crucifixion, I believe that God allows and encourages governments to 'wield the sword' to maintain peace and restrain evil so long as we live in a world where Jesus is not yet recognized as Lord. The Gospel brings in the Kingdom of God but we do not yet see everything under His rule; in the meantime Satan is active because he knows his time is short. I believe that his activity may sometimes have to be resisted by legitimate force, exercised by God-ordained rulers acting in a legal capacity just as a policeman has the right to use force in his official capacity and not just as an expression of personal spite; even so, governments have the right to use the minimum force required to maintain a just peace.

With regard to the problem created in some minds by the military structure of officers and other ranks, it seems to me that Paul, in his letter to the church at Ephesus, lays down principles with regard to the master and slave relationship which are intensely practical for modern living. I think of one Christian fellowship in the headquarters of B.A.O.R. where all ranks met happily together to pray. Unfortunately one young lady Lance Corporal had not yet grasped the Bible teaching on this aspect of life and greeted her commanding officer (the head of police) by his Christian name when he was escorting the Chief of the Imperial General Staff from London on the day following the meetings.

The army needs Christian men and women to act as salt and leaven as much as any other profession, and my experience during my tours of army units as a Christian has convinced me that although it is difficult to hold to the faith firmly and graciously in the forces, it is by no means impossible; and many have seen that true Christianity gives an extra dimension to leadership and man-management which is in itself a commendable testimony to Christ.

On my most recent visit to the army, a brigade mission in Northern Ireland, the spiritual crisis was brought very clearly into focus. Ten days before the mission was due to start, six soldiers had been bombed when taking part in a marathon in what was formerly considered a safe area. Their comrades in the brigade were not only shattered by this event (although some were as a consequence more open to spiritual reality) but hardened towards the terrorists, so that any suggestion of forgiveness was treated with contempt and utter lack of understanding. If the troubles have hardened the Irish they have also hardened the soldiers, who need constantly to be on the alert and who are only too aware of the minority, including the six-to-ten-year-old stone-throwing children, of the surrounding population who have a very deep hatred towards them. To maintain efficiency and love under such circumstances takes divine grace, and the witness of the few committed Christians in any garrison is very obvious. I was deeply impressed with some of the Christian officers, N.C.O.'s and men that I met. Many of them were young in the faith but bright in their witness both of life and Word.

I have been privileged to take part in the officers' Christian Union Ski House-Party on three occasions. Young officers and cadets from Sandhurst attend for two weeks before Christmas. The activity is encouraged by the college and it is known that the organizers are Christian. To teach under such circumstances is a tremendous privilege. Young, fit, intelligent, co-ordinated and highly-motivated young men and women take to snow like a duck to water, but the greatest privilege was to be able to use the relationship established on the slopes to communicate the Gospel both on those slopes and at the informal meetings held each evening.

If Germany and Northern Ireland have been connected with my service in the army of both the

Queen and King Jesus, the two other trips abroad which I have been privileged to enjoy have been exclusively concerned with the spiritual. University Presbyterian Church in Seattle, Washington, U.S.A., had sent four young people to assist in summer missions in Scotland for a number of years as part of their summer deputation programme, sending out teams to at least six areas throughout the world. The First Presbyterian Church in Fresno, California, had been involved in the 'Along-side Ministry', providing opportunities for young people to work alongside local churches on a reciprocal basis throughout the world. In 1982 I was asked to speak at the Seekers' Conference (associated with Alongside Ministries) and to visit Lee and Dottie Dale who chaired the deputation committee of the United Presbyterian Church. Joy and our two youngest children accompanied me for what had originally been intended as mainly a holiday but turned into a visit when I was asked to speak at least once per day during the nineteen-day stay.

The warmth and welcome of the American Church has to be experienced to be believed and we spent a memorable three weeks being feasted, shown round, and generally feted. On the spiritual side two things struck me very forcibly, and although it is exceedingly unwise to generalize after one brief stay perhaps these two are worth mentioning. The first was the sheer size, efficiency and wealth of American churches compared with those in Scotland. Enthusiasm for and quality in all that was done in the name of Jesus put us to shame, although we were somewhat mesmerized by a staff of fifty-six full-time workers, including a High School section of two full-time and one part-time worker for sixteen-to-eighteen youngsters! The whole scale of the operation was in danger of causing envy, but two incidents put this into perspective. I was asked to a missionary breakfast and in the course of conversation discovered that the church supported almost one hundred missionaries on the fields of the world. But I also discovered that not one came from that actual church, and that local evangelism in the downtown area around the church building was carried out by an outside organization paid to do the task by the committee. That evening the elder with whom we stayed confided that he was fearful lest business efficiency had usurped the place of spiritual reality in the lives of many in the church.

The second feature which I noticed centred around Christian teaching. In one of the churches there was a magnificent system of all-age Christian education, using extremely attractive materials. I noticed, however, that the starting point was always a current issue or some aspect of human need, and this was brought home to me as we drove back to Seattle from the Seekers' Conference. I had taken three Biblical passages which seemed to feature in the title of 'This is The Day' that had been given to me. We looked at 'This is The Day the Lord has made', 'Today is the day of salvation' and 'As you see the day approaching', and I had sought simply to expound the Scriptures. The assistant minister who was acting as my chauffeur spoke appreciatively as we drove back and commented, 'That was the Gospel. We never get things from the Bible like that'. Perhaps it is not only in the States that we need to start with Scripture - and stay with it.

But what a joy it was to worship in such a company, and to share fellowship with so many warm-hearted and gorgeous Christians for whom nothing seemed to be too much trouble. We were taken to a beach house on the Pacific, to the restaurant at the top of the circulating tower overlooking all Seattle, to the ski grounds of Washington and California, and to the magnificent mountains and canyons of Yosemite as well as the modern marvel of Los Angeles. Memories of a huge swimming pool in the garden and of hundreds of tons of peaches being prepared for Marks and Spencers will remain in the mind; but above all, the feeling of love and acceptance by fellow Christians who opened their homes and their hearts to us as if to the Lord Himself.

This warm Christian fellowship across all the barriers of culture is surely one of the thrills of the Christian life, and can be experienced in Scotland, Northern Ireland, Germany, America or Africa, it matters not where.

A Malawian student for the ministry had asked to come on the Speyside summer mission whilst staying in Edinburgh to study. He was a most valuable member of the team and appreciated his stay with us, but I was not altogether prepared for the invitation I received from him a year later to come to Malawi with Scotroc and lead a three-week mission to the Livingstonia Synod of the Church of Central Africa Presbyterians. After much prayer and discussion it was felt we should accept the invitation, and plans were prepared, which included a prayerful looking to God for provision of the £6,000 needed to meet all expenses.

As the date in July approached, financial needs had been met in a quite remarkable way, and flight transport had been booked, when I heard that my African friend had been struck by lightning and was off work, virtually in a coma. What was God's plan in all this? Should we go or cancel? We were given conflicting advice but eventually it was decided that we should meet with the general secretary of the Synod, who was due to visit Scotland that very week, and accept his decision. I met him at Edinburgh airport, and after a short rest he met all the team, who were giving a Gospel concert in Dunfermline that night. After prayer and discussion together he listened to the Gospel presentation, which must have been totally foreign to his culture. Afterwards he met us briefly and said, 'I am not sure what you have to give my people but you should come'. We did!

On arrival at Lilongwe airport we had to pass through customs and immigration before waiting for a flight to Mzuzu. As I spoke with the customs officer he greeted me with a warm smile. 'Brother, we have been praying for you, and will continue to do so throughout the mission'. What a welcome, still many hundreds of miles from our destination!

We arrived at Mzuzu in the early evening, exhausted by the journey, only to be told that there was a special service that night in the church. Over one thousand people crowded into a building designed for three hundred, and we had our first taste of African worship and hunger for the Word of God as the meeting went on for many hours, with several preachers (including myself) expected to preach for not less than forty-five minutes each.

And so started a memorable three weeks. Malawi is well-named the warm heart of Africa but warmth and efficiency are not always synonymous, and it was an experience for us Europeans to be told to be ready at 8 a.m. and then have the Land Rover eventually set out at 3.30 p.m. Time has a different meaning in that country, and sometimes we arrived to speak to groups who had waited for up to nine hours without any complaint. Length of services, too, varied somewhat from the Scottish time limit. On our second day there was an open-air rally for the Synod, starting at eight o'clock on Sunday morning. Some five thousand folk had gathered from up to fifty miles walk away, and the second of two services was drawing to a close at eleven o'clock when I was passed a note asking me to preach at 11.30. Twenty minutes preparation time for one hour's exposition! Things were never like this in Scotland! Eventually the rally ended at 3.30 in the afternoon as most of the participants had to walk home for work on the Monday morning. Before they left, many hundreds were drawn to Christ and counselled.

The team consisted of two young men and three girls, and their music and drama was greatly appreciated: indeed, one song, called 'Empty Handed', became so popular that it was demanded on very occasion and became our theme song. It was a great favourite of Hastings, our interpreter, who became a most enthusiastic member of the team. Sometimes he was stuck for a word but nothing daunted him. We saw some of the missionaries smile broadly on one occasion, and later realized that he had translated the words of the chorus 'Ascribe greatness to our God the rock' as 'A big secretary to our God the stone!'

Culture shock was experienced by most members of the team (one ate remarkably little during the whole of our three-week stay) and a certain theological shock caused me a few problems, especially when teaching at the youth conference in Livingstone. We had agreed to a consecutive line of teaching with our African co-leaders and then found the subjects and their order had become mixed up. I was scheduled to speak on the same subject in the afternoon as had been covered in the morning, and some things said by one teacher were contradicted by the next. But Christian grace prevailed and God used the conference, despite us, to touch the hearts of hundreds of young folk who had gathered for the occasion.

We spent some time with the missionaries sent out by the Church of Scotland and others, and it was a time of encouragement for them too. They are under the authority of the local church, and that it is not always the easiest situation to be in but it was good to see the Spirit of Jesus finding ways through situations which would otherwise have been impossible.

There were memorable moments: swimming in Lake Malawi, and one of the team suffering from extreme sunburn as a result; travelling miles in the back of a Land Rover with thick red dust everywhere; arriving at an encampment occupied apparently only by monkeys to find a two-and-a-half hour official welcome by the evangelist, district government officer, and tribal chief, arranged at virtually no notice, whilst a congregation of three hundred gathered, as if by magic, some from twenty miles away. These memories will not quickly fade, but the abiding impression was of a people as warm as their beautiful country, and a hunger for the Word of God which thrilled the soul. This made the transition to the somewhat dour situation which greeted us on our return to Britain somewhat hard to bear.

Chapter 11

WHERE ARE WE GOING?

Persuaded by a number of Christian friends whom I held in high regard, I had decided in August 1987 that God was calling me to retire from my work as the evangelist of the Church of Scotland. I was leading the last scheduled mission with Scotroc in Larbert and looking forward to that retirement in our new home in Kincraig when a phone call from Edinburgh started a chain of events which led to a complete change of plan. God works in mysterious ways. I had known David Anderson since he was at University, and on one occasion had to leave his rooms by the window at 2.00am, when a fire alarm found me in the residence after hours. We had a close affinity of spirit as God had given us both a deep concern for revival and a desire to see the Word of the Lord faithfully proclaimed and obeyed throughout our land.

His phone call was to ask if I were to be in Edinburgh in the near future, and I was able to tell him that I was due there in two days and would be free for lunch. After our meal he started to describe the ways in which God had led him and the small leadership group of Gorgie church to seek extra staff, and even as he began I knew that the person they had in mind was myself.

As he unfolded the story and described the many apparent 'coincidences' which pointed to myself, and ended with a rough job description that I might have written myself, I sensed that God was clearly behind the call. But we had just sold Alltnacriche to the Scripture Union and bought a smaller house in Kincraig; I had also recently been accepted as the Honourary Missions Advisor for Universities and Colleges Christian Fellowship in Scotland, and was becoming increasingly involved in the establishment of prayer breakfasts, mainly for men, in every government agency of 'Concern for Scotland'. The future had seemed so settled and straightforward that my immediate reaction was 'God, why can't You leave me alone?'

David and I prayed, and I went back to the mission at Larbert with very mixed feelings. One thing was quite clear in my mind: my wife had to be of the same conviction if this move was truly of God. After sharing and prayer together, for many days, it was clear that God was calling us to Gorgie for three or four years, and so another phase began to emerge.

The move was delayed until the Spring and so a final winter of ski teaching with Abernethy on Cairngorm gave some opportunity to be involved in God's setting up of 'Concern for Scotland' prayer groups in many districts of the land. This movement had its origin four years previously when five of us had spontaneously come together with a deep concern for the spiritual state of Scotland and an awareness of the need for unity across denominational and other barriers. After years of meeting together in a group which gradually increased in size, it became apparent that God was not calling for some sort of evangelical alliance in Scotland to plan and co-ordinate evangelism and associated activities, but rather for local groups to meet together in prayer for the revival of the nation through a spiritual revival in the church. We became aware that combined activity normally excludes, and can cause division, but that prayer unites, and brings about a situation where activity may be prompted by the Spirit. We have a horror of new organisations or a multiplicity of meetings and are simply seeking to encourage and co-ordinate the mounting swell of prayer across the land. Part of this is by the sending out of a national prayer bulletin.

The move to Edinburgh was not easy, especially for Joy. The wife, of necessity, sees the home as her base, and to have two homes and loyalties to two communities was a great emotional strain; but when God calls, He also gives all necessary grace, although entry into a state of joyful acceptance may take some time. For me, a settled ministry has many attractions; but in many ways it takes me back twenty years - going into a new situation with no clear guidelines - because my call to Gorgie is to be the associate minister with primary responsibilities for evangelism and teaching, yet also to be set free to go as the Lord directs throughout the land. It is always more difficult to be under the direction of the Spirit than of some institution or organisation.

From this privileged position I look out on Scotland from the warm and welcoming community of Gorgie and begin to see even more clearly God's purpose for His Church and mission in these coming days. The picture clears and fades, like the hills through an early morning mist as the sun shines and then hides gloomily behind the dark swirling masses of vapour, but always the mists lessen and the sun grows stronger.

For many years I have had a strong conviction that God will act in judgement against our land and especially against the Church, where judgement must always begin. The sheer immorality and acceptance of injustice in the nation and the utter unbelief of the Church call alike for God to come in His just wrath. 'It is time for the Lord to act because His law is being broken', says Psalm 119 at verse 126.

I have often stated, in recent years, the realisation that I am unlikely to die in my bed, but in a jail - for my faith. Political and philosophical polarisation has reached the point where the middle ground has collapsed and totalitarianism of extreme right or extreme left looms nearer as year succeeds year. The prophetic voice of judgement is seldom heard in our land, and when it is, it falls upon highly unwilling ears and hard hearts. Is there a word from the Lord, and is it of doom and gloom? I believe with all my heart that the answer is yes, - but that there is hope!. The apparent contradiction is perhaps only in our rational minds, controlled by fallen logic. The Scriptures find no contradiction in wrath and revival going hand in hand, and the longing and expectation of many godly men throughout the centuries since Christ is for revival in the midst of persecution. Perhaps the Puritans had the clearest vision of this hope shining in and through apparent disaster.

Jeremiah faithfully proclaimed God's message of defeat, capitulation and captivity to an unbelieving people but at the same time purchased property and secured the deeds for the certainty of the future. In his case some seventy years separated judgement from revival or the captivity from the restoration; but from the perspective of eternity, time is often telescoped, and it would seem from the forecasting of events in the last days that judgement and revival may well accompany each other, rather than the one precede the other. The prophet Habakkuk foresaw economic and religious collapse, living with lips quivering at the sound of enemy action, and with legs trembling; and yet he held on to the conviction of ultimate triumph. Let me bring it up to date. Would he have written along these lines today?

'Though the FT index falls below two hundred,
And the pound's as little value as the yen:
Though the gun and truncheon rule in all our cities,
And the Jackboot struts as far as the lonely glen:
Though AIDS and heroin addiction spread, though terror will not wait,
For Priest and Judge are firmly muzzled by the state:
Yet I will rejoice in the Lord,
I will be joyful in God my Saviour'.

There are so many signs of a society sick, divided and ready for disintegration, with a Church uncertain, compromised with ecclesiastical power politics and in-fighting; yet there are signs of hope as more and more individuals and groups are humbled and brought to their knees before God in prayer. A rising tide of prayer and expectation is beginning to move in our land. There are those who say that revival has already come as I write these words in 1988. But let us beware lest we fall into the trap foreseen in the parable of the supercar.

'A British manufacturer had finally perfected the family supercar, and the launch was planned for October that year. The secret was leaked in the Spring, and two rival foreign firms rushed out a counterfeit by September. Huge publicity ensured vast sales, but the only too obvious faults of the new model ensured that when the genuine article finally came on to the market it was spurned and ignored'.

Our hope and expectation is real revival - not just 'revival of religion' but revival of character, life and society-changing dimensions: that revival which changes not only individuals but the whole thinking and structure of society. Many are starting to pray. My hope and conviction is that the tide of prayer will deepen and grow, until it flows into the outpouring of God's Spirit upon western civilization, through the Church, in a mighty flood:

> 'While now the tired waves vainly breaking
> Seem here no painful inch to gain,
> Far back through creeks and inlet making,
> Comes silent, flooding in, the main'.

After the spiritual contest on Mount Carmel, Elijah heard the sound of rain by the ear of faith. He sent his servant to look for the token of what was to come, and six times the man returned with a totally negative report. On the seventh occasion he reported a cloud 'like a man's hand'. Elijah saw this as the certain token of the thunder to come and, after warning the king, ran the half marathon to the capital city in front of him. That cloud is on the horizon in Scotland today. The rain has not yet come but perhaps a few drops are beginning to fall. Let us not, in our zeal and enthusiasm, exaggerate those drops into the storm, but let us not lose the certainty of faith which sees those drops as the sure harbinger of an outpouring of God Himself.

I wonder will I see it through the prison bars, or could it come in time to save us from God's righteous judgement? All I do know, with absolute certainty, is that Jesus is Lord and one glorious day will demonstrate that fact. The world will see, acknowledge and bow the knee.

As I conclude this story of what God has done in my insignificant life, I would ask you, reader - will you be among those who are forced to acknowledge Him when He comes, or will you surrender to Him now and join those who are eagerly and joyfully awaiting His coming?